Presented to

Silas Rhodes

with Gratitude, Respect
and Affection by

Milton Stier

Tales from the Light

Milton J. Stier

I dedicate this work to four people:

To my devoted helpmate, my severest critic, my nurse, and my beloved bride of 63 years, my Selma.

To the two people who conceived of this volume and made it a reality: My exuberant and enthusiastic niece, Joanne Schlichter, editor par excellence who made it come to life.
My wise and compassionate daughter, Emily Stier Adler, Ph.D., who gave me so much pride and pleasure because she "did it all": career, home, husband and children.

And to my father and first teacher, Josef Stier, who took his family out of the reach of the Holocaust and provided a role model for me to emulate, if not achieve. Although he has been dead for 33 years, his influence still fills my life.

Acknowledgement

I would like to thank Dr. Jerome Yarett and Herbert Adise, who valiantly struggled with me to sustain my temple's magazine, *The Light,* where most of these pieces were originally published. My thanks as well to Leonard Abrams, who did all of the technical work for the magazine and who helped me make *The Light* the prestigious magazine it is today. My appreciation goes to Rona Lupkin, the temple librarian, who helped me locate many of these stories. Thanks are also due to Lauren Lickus for her fine work in doing the layout that turned stories from a magazine into a book. Last and most, I thank the clergy, especially Rabbi Waxman, and the staff and members of congregation Temple Israel of Great Neck, my *goldene medinah,* for supporting the magazine. They gave me a wonderful intellectual toy as well as the status of being editor-in-chief to bolster my ego.

About the Author

Milton Josef Stier was born in 1919 in Czernovitz, Bukovina, then part of Austro-Hungry, the first born of Josef and Molly Stier. He immigrated to the United States with his parents as child. His childhood was spent his childhood in Brooklyn and the Bronx with his two younger siblings, Murray and Gladys.

As a boy, he often worked with his parents in their kosher butcher shop. After graduating from high school at 16, he opened his own kosher butcher store before going to work for General Motors in Tarrytown, NY, where he rose to the position of foreman. Volunteering for service during World War II, he was stationed in France and Germany, serving first as a tank driver in the armed corps and then as an interpreter and interrogator of military and political prisoners in Germany.

Before leaving for overseas duty, he and Selma Schwartz were married in January of 1945.

After the war, Milton worked in a variety of occupations before going into the field of education. He started a potting soil business and a plastic toy factory and later became a shoe salesman. Together with his wife Selma and his brother- and sister-in-law Helen and Jerry Schlichter, he also built and ran Camp Brydon Lake in the Catskills from 1947 to 1962.

Milton attended City College in the evenings, but he received his B.A. and M.A. from New York University. He worked first as an elementary school teacher and then as a social sciences teacher in the New York City public school system, while also teaching English as a second language in the evenings from 1948 to 1962. Moving into administration, he served as an assistant principal and then principal at nine different schools. His last full-time job in education was as community superintendent in one of the most difficult school districts in the Bronx. In 1970, he received his doctorate in education from New York University, writing his dissertation on the effects of local control of community school districts in New York City.

After his official retirement, he continued to work in the field of education. He trained candidates for the position of principal and served as a hearing officer in discipline cases for the New York City school system. He also became actively involved in adult education, lecturing to community groups on a variety of topics, including history and current events. In addition, he served on the board of trustees of the School of Visual Arts for over 25 years.

As a member of Temple Israel of Great Neck for over 50 years, Milton served in many roles. He was an usher at services, chair of the education committee, and president of the Minyanaires, a Sunday morning study group. He enjoyed a long and close friendship with both Rabbi Mordecai Waxman and Dr. Ruth Waxman of blessed memory.

Milton's most significant activity at Temple Israel was to serve for 36 years as a contributor and then editor-in-chief of *The Light,* the synagogue's highly regarded literary magazine. He enjoyed writing the many stories and articles that *The Light* published. He had a regular column of wit and humor in the magazine, published under the name Kunye Lemel. Many of the stories in this collection were originally published in *The Light*.

In addition to writing, Milton's hobbies are varied. Over the years he has enjoyed photography, ceramics, travel, folk dancing, bridge, baking and gardening.

Milton has two children, Emily and Gordon, a son-in-law George and a daughter-in-law Beth, and three grandchildren, Josh, Rebecca and Jessica. He values family connections and considers it both a duty and a privilege to keep in touch with nieces, nephews and other members of his extended family scattered in cities all over the world, including Toronto, Milan, Tel Aviv, Haifa, San Francisco, London and Santiago.

Contents

Introduction

Why did I want to publish my writings as a book?

Mainly as a way to share my memories with my family, I suppose. As I have gotten older, I have realized that despite medical advances, the death rate has not changed. It is still one per person. But each death is never a mere statistic. Each death tears the fabric of a family. Part of the family's group memory is erased—forever. This book is designed to fill that future gap and preserve my memories as part of my family's heritage.

Are these tales true?

I don't know! Over the decades I have written them and told them and added to them to the point where they have taken on a life of their own. As this project involved a great deal of recall, I had to unearth many stories—some of them 50 years old. I blush to report that most of them seemed fresh and enjoyable to me.

Some of these pieces are clearly marked as fiction: "The Fiddle," "The Girl with the Gloves," "The Interview," "Weekend Pass," "Awaiting the Messenger," "Old Buddy". Even those, however, have a kernel of my own life as the starting point. In two essays, "Déjà Vu" and "My Father Is a Jewish Mother," I wrote in my son's voice in order to convey my own experiences as a father.

But while all of these tales, fictional and non-fictional, have some biographical content, they have been stretched, augmented and exaggerated to the point that I have lost the boundary separating truth from fiction.

My parents had similar problems. My father would boast, "I can clearly remember events from 30 or 40 years ago." My mother would respond, "You remember things that never happened!"

So, good reader, seek not unalloyed truth, but understand that I never allowed cold facts to interfere with a joke or a good yarn. And if you enjoyed these tales, please let me know by e-mailing me at MiltonStier@Yahoo.com.

Milton Stier

Growing Up

Red Gold

He was the most unJewish Jew I ever knew. He stood well over six feet tall, about 240 pounds, built like a bullock, with not an inch of fat on him anywhere. He rarely spoke below a bellow and moved with the violent power of a bulldozer. Topping off his massive frame was a shock of brilliant but untidy red hair. Since his legal name was Yakov Gold, the name "Red" Gold was obvious.

He was one of my father's competitors. My father was a successful meat dealer, though he thought this occupation was beneath him. He owned and operated several stores. These were sometimes free-standing stores, but most often a stand within a public market, where each stand—fruit, meat, fish, and so on— was rented and operated by separate owners who shared the costs of the common areas. One such public market was large enough to accommodate two of each kind of stand, and that is how Red Gold entered my life. He ran a kosher meat stand in the same market as my father and they were business rivals.

Red Gold was a fearsome man, especially to a frail ten-year-old, like me. The area around him was always in constant turmoil. He would stand, wearing a soiled apron and waving a knife or cleaver, while he cursed and yelled affectionate names at his customers. Most customers feared him, yet were fascinated by his earthy vitality. He would spend the day laughing, bellowing and doing the work of two normal men. I recall, with admiration, how he could lift a whole side of beef, about 200 pounds, to his shoulder and then stand conversing with a worker, without any sign of strain.

He could wield a cleaver and a knife with the grace of a ballet dancer, yet his general movements were as a graceless as a pig on ice. His wife, a very beautiful woman who had the blackest hair I had ever seen, had all of the grace in the family. At a time when few women worked outside of the home, she stood alongside her titanic husband, acting as the cashier and general overseer. I always thought of her as Mrs. Gold, because not only did I not know her first name, but in those days, children never called adults by their first name. She rarely cut meat, but I knew she could expertly split a lamb with a cleaver. Although he towered over her, Red always spoke to her with quiet respect and guarded his tongue, which was often given to vulgarity. Once, when she lost her temper over a minor discrepancy and flew at him, I realized why he, big as he was, backed away from her in fear.

As I look back, I realize that I was always entranced by them, by their mannerisms, their behavior and how different they were from "regular" people.

It was rumored, and probably correctly, that he kept a jug of whiskey in his butcher's icebox from which he took a frequent nip to ward off the cold. It was also rumored that he had killed a man with one blow of his fist, and that he had escaped punishment by the intervention of his brother, who was a *starker* [enforcer] for the local politically connected gang. Childishly, I had altered that story so that in my overheated imagination, he had killed the man in his icebox and then, using his skills with knife and saw, had dismembered the victim and sold him as chopped meat. It was obvious that my free-ranging imagination had been corrupted by the Gothic horror tales I had read so avidly.

It was only natural that a man like Red Gold would quarrel with his neighbors. One day he found fault with my father and with loud cries of rage and threats of instant annihilation, he raced over to our end of the market to confront my father. All of the other storekeepers scattered.

My father also was an atypical Jew. He had served as an officer in the Austrian army for eight years and had received four medals for bravery, two of which were pinned on him by the Austrian emperor himself. While he was only of average height, my father could dominate any room, because he had the light grey-green eyes of a stone cold killer. Many times I had seen big, noisy, and violent men grow quiet in his presence. Except for one incident over a straw hat, I had never seen my father strike another man. He didn't seem to need to. They treated him with the careful respect one gives a truly dangerous gunslinger.

Red Gold charged over, waving his cleaver and demanding satisfaction for some utterly nonsensical grievance. My father stood looking at him quietly, but let his hand fall lightly to the handle of his own cleaver. Red Gold paused, well out of arm's reach, and fulminated and bellowed, while my father stood silent and unmoved. Eventually, even this Bull of Bashan lost some of his steam. As his wife led him away, he muttered, "You should be glad that I can control my temper." My father's response thrilled me. "No. You should be glad you controlled yourself." Red never challenged him again and would go out of his way to show him respect. My father ignored his overtures. After all, why deal with a Crimean Cossack from Odessa, a *balaugoula* [common laborer]?

I was still enthralled by the Golds and would pass their stand and covertly observe them whenever I could. He ignored me, but she would smile as though she knew what I was thinking.

I don't know how this came about, but there was a wedding in the community to which both families were invited. There I met the four Gold children, two boys, one with red hair, the other with black hair and two girls similarly colored. My mother called them the checkerboard children and my father called them the "Stendhals." It was not until college that I understood that he was referring to the title of Stendhals' work, *The Red and the Black*. Where my father, who rarely read a book in my presence, got that literary allusion, I'll never know.

That wedding was where, at the age of twelve, I fell in love with Mrs. Gold. During the dancing most of the dancers proceeded with ungainly but sedate waltz steps, but Mrs. Gold flung her hair loose and danced a gypsy flamenco. She was stamping and twirling, while singing loudly, in a husky sexy voice, the wholly inappropriate American song, "Yes Sir, She's my Baby Now." Every woman present was aghast and every man fascinated. When the Golds danced together with wild abandon, the floor shuddered and the people cheered, and the dance floor was hastily cleared in admiration and fear. It was obvious from the way they danced and looked at each other that despite their raucous speech and vulgar manners, this was a love match, not an arranged marriage.

I could not take my eyes off of them. They seemed so full of life, so much larger than life, that I thought they would simply explode with life force. While in the background, I could hear my mother saying *paskutzveh* [disgusting] and *shande* [shameful], I was thinking of how wonderful it would be to have a mate like that. I realized that much of my dislike of Red was based on envy. I speculatively looked at the older of the two Gold girls, about my age. Even though she smiled back, I knew my father would never let me be friends with a daughter of the Golds.

I thought, as children do, that all adults were old people, but both the Golds and my parents were only in their thirties. So it was a shock to the community when Red Gold, working in his icebox, suddenly died of a heart attack. His life style, his drinking, and severe daily physical exertion had taken their toll. My mother, trying to console the distraught Mrs. Gold, said, "He was burning his candle too fast."

Mrs. Gold, with the aid of her brother-in-law, made a feeble attempt to keep the store running, but despite my father's assistance, it was an obvious impossibility. So she sold out. The family moved away and I never saw any of them again.

But they left me with an indelible reminder that Jews are not alike and that amongst us are those not destined to be quiet Yeshiva *buchers* [seminary students], but those able to burst the bonds of routine and to pursue an undisciplined life of the physical senses. His was a life filled with zest, gaiety, song and labor.

Red was a kind of person who helped the Jews survive, a model for Jewish success in the rough-and-tumble world of business. Though he inspired me with fear and dislike, above all, I felt admiration.

Shlugim Nicht in Kup

My father did not hit us often, but when he did it was a most memorable occasion. He knowingly violated the rule that thou shalt not strike your child in anger. He always struck us in anger. Otherwise, what was the purpose? He thought, and I agree now, that to promise to punish you later and then quietly and dispassionately administer punishment was cruel, because it added the anxiety of waiting to the pain of the blows. I think such taught responses by parents tend to poison the atmosphere more than a blow struck in the heat of the moment.

My father never told us that "this hurts me more than it does you." First, because he wouldn't lie to us. Second, because there was very little conversation before the blow landed.

It was your responsibility to be sensitive enough to know that he was reaching the flashpoint of his rather short temper. His blow always left a rather angry red mark, because he thought enough of us to give us his very best. In his later years, my father vehemently denied ever striking any of his children. He sincerely believed this. He was aghast that I should accuse him of such an unfeeling practice. His children were such good children that he never had any need to punish them. He was right in a way. He was not punishing us, he was simply using the most direct means of instruction available. After trying reason, which would often fail with over-exuberant children, he would become impatient (as I said, he had a very short fuse)

28

and would apply his psychology directly to the nearest part of the anatomy.

These scenes always upset my mother. She would hover on the outskirts of conflict, never daring to interfere directly, murmuring phrases such as "nebee ataw," which I believe was a Roumanian or Hungarian version of *rachmones* [mercy], and the admonition, "*Shlugim nicht in kup*" [Don't hit him in the head]. My mother was sure that head blows would make us stupid, the worst handicap for a Jewish boy. I really can't blame my father for my lack of ability because I managed to dodge most of his blows.

It was good strategy to start howling before any of the blows actually landed, because this sometimes inhibited the assault. So you could see my father flailing at a rapidly dodging, circling and howling progeny. Our natural and learned agility kept us from serious harm, as did the fact that my father cooled as rapidly as he ignited.

It is interesting that my mother never hit us. She relied on *knipping* [pinching]. She could squeeze a cheek or an arm like a nutcracker to get our attention and our obedience. Then she would call in the heavy battalions; she would tell Papa what we had done. He would react in his usual strong fashion and she would be horrified by the result. After he hit us, she would sooth our hurt, never noting that she herself had paradoxically created the whole stormy scene. While we did not enjoy these hectic and noisy events, they tended to brighten and spice up the rather humdrum routine of eat, sleep, work and school.

A more important break in the weekday routine occurred on Sunday. Then the family car (an object of envy among our Pitkin Avenue neighbors) would take us to a lovely and lonely spot on the outskirts of the city for a picnic. As we drove, the children, all seated in the back (the front was always reserved for adults), started their usual teasing and fooling around with constant cries of "Papa, he is bothering me." This tumult annoyed my father and he would stop the car in the middle of the highway (traffic was much lighter in the Twenties), open the rear door, and administer a blow to each of the children in turn. He was impartial and uninterested in the cause and a great believer that collective punishment tended to create collective responsibility. I noticed that he was gentleman enough to give my sister less than he gave the boys.

This would work for all of five minutes and then the back seat became alive with giggles, shoves and cries, as we vied for window seats. Then the car would stop and the whole episode was repeated. This gave our vehicle a rather spasmodic method of passage that rightly belonged to the Keystone Comedies we so enjoyed.

When we reached the picnic area, we would all eat and my father would "rest his eyes." For some reason he always denied that he slept on such family gatherings because that appeared to him to be a sign of weakness, but he really did sleep.

My mother would repack the food containers and sit on the blanket, waving the children away for fear they would awaken Papa. We were free to do anything, except make noise, climb trees, run, get dirty or go out of sight. Mama knew that if Papa were aroused from his "non-sleeping," the trip home would be ruined by his constant mutterings of phrases such as "For whom am I working?" or "For whom am I giving my life's blood?" or "For whom am I killing myself?" and so on. The children really didn't mind, because the monotonous litany and the traffic noises soon lulled them to sleep as well.

The only other time my father took off was on Saturday, the Sabbath. He was a hard worker and good provider, so it was my mother's obligation and our duty not to disturb his rest during that day.

Thus on Saturday morning, Mama would feed us as quickly and as quietly as possible, pack an enormous lunch for all, and send us off to the movies by 9 a.m. We would head for the local cinema, called "kin-ee-mah" by the local residents, where we would join the throngs streaming in to view the latest chapter of the exciting serials, like the "Sign of the Frog" or the "Mark of Zorro." Many of these caused nightmares later, but who could resist seeing them? Sometimes we would view the scary parts crouched down behind our seats, a clear indication of how real these shadow plays had become to us.

We would wait on line with our noisy and unruly friends until 11 a.m. when the mob of "patrons" was permitted to enter. We would tumultuously greet the familiar faces that grimaced at us from the silent screen. Maybe the screen was silent, but the audience certainly was not. For five to fifteen cents, depending on the time or the neighborhood, one could become part of the happy throng, eating, shrieking, running to the toilets, and rolling soda bottles down the aisle. (Matrons were a thing of the far distant future). Everyone read the titles aloud to show off their reading skills.

The noise was horrendous. No adults came during these sessions, they didn't have the nerves for it. The piercing howl that arose when a series chapter or a cartoon comedy started was strong enough to bring down an ICBM in full flight.

After three full-length features, several cartoons, a comedy, serial chapters, a newsreel and endless coming attractions, we would stumble out into the late afternoon Brooklyn sunshine.

The scenery looked weird to us after swimming on Mars, hiding from varnpires in dark castles, or chasing Indians down Monument Valley.

While we would have liked to have stayed for a repeat of one or two examples of cinematic art, dilatory children made Mama worry and that brought on Papa's heavy-handed instructional process on punctuality. When we got home, we found Mama had caught up on her endless chores and Papa was relaxed.

We explained the intricacies of the plots to our parents and found them profoundly uninterested in our somewhat incoherent resumés. They found most such things, in fact, anything not directly related to health, business, family, home furnishings, and similar vital necessities, to be simply *narishkeit* [foolishness]. While they read newspapers, they never read books, because those were not related to family survival and they had no time to waste on such meaningless trivia. Hence they rarely went to the movies themselves because they found them inane and childish.

My father's impatience with what he thought of as childish nonsense was most frequently displayed at the dinner table. We could tell when he was close to anger by his expression.

He felt the time at the table should be devoted to eating and listening—to him. He would show his irritability at our noise, inattention or quarrelling, by giving us terrifying sidelong glances. Not even Medusa could produce such a chilling visage. He would say, "Look in your plate." That meant "shut up," "watch out" or "you are going to catch it." Strangely enough, this often worked in a contrary fashion. The fear and trepidation that this evoked caused us to burst into nervous giggles. This provoked hysterical laughter from our siblings. Then, as Papa continued to glower, our fits of laughter became more explosive. We would stuff our napkins into our mouths in the hopeless effort to quell the laughs. Finally, we would plunge away from the table, without permission, because Papa was close to ignition by this time.

Somehow the blows, the tirades, and the sermons never seemed to change our relationship with Papa. He could always be calmed if you weren't fresh, the ultimate offense in his mind. This meant waiting quietly until the storm blew over and never, never, never correcting him, even if you knew he was wrong. You were not permitted to complain that he was unfair. You were permitted to cry as long as it was of reasonable duration and intensity. He hated to think you could not control yourself.

We seem to have suffered few scars on our psyches, and none on our bodies as a result of Papa's tactics. We all grew up, married Jews, raised families, have no divorces and made decent careers in spite of this "cruel" regime.

We thought that all parents loved their children enough to give them a few whacks once in a while. We were too secure in our affection for, and affection from, Papa to realize that he had violated our civil rights. We intuitively realized that a household where parents are not strong and respected figures was not a safe and secure haven for children. The wrath and strength he displayed towards us kept the evils of the world at bay. He was a tiger, but he was our tiger.

The Coal Chute
Rashomon Variations in Brooklyn

Memory does not always serve us well. Here are four differing versions of the same event. Which rings most true?

Version One

In the wilds of Brooklyn in the wilder times of my extreme youth, my father owned a small building. It was not the sort of structure calculated to make Donald Trump grow envious. It nestled under the roaring elevated subway line (an oxymoron if there ever was one), better known as the Pitkin Avenue El, and contained the grand total of three apartments, known as railroad flats, over a small retail store.

My father was not only the landlord or *lendler*, a grand title for a recent immigrant, but he was also the tenant of the store, and our family lived in the first-floor apartment. It was in that apartment that we learned how to punctuate our conversations with 27 seconds of silence, as the trains hurtled and roared by at the height of our windows on a regular basis. It gave our conversation a sort of Morse code effect, but it made for more useful speech patterns because time was essential and one needed to organize one's thoughts rapidly or else suffer interruption. The silences gave one the opportunity to revise a previous statement or to blame the train for a previous misinterpretation: "You didn't hear that right because the train was so noisy."

Because the building did not have that modern advance, central heating, it received coal deliveries on a regular basis for use in the large kitchen coal stoves in each flat. This coal arrived in a massive truck and would be sent crashing down into coal bins in the cellar via a chute set into the sidewalk. We had no fancy basements in those days.

The coal chute was covered by a small manhole cover that was kept locked to avoid a passerby falling in. The heavy brass key to this cover was kept in the cellar and someone in the family, usually me, was assigned to wait for the truck and open the chute so the coal man could pour his black gold into the cellar.

One day I received the assignment to await the coal man immediately after school. I promptly forgot and engaged in a thrilling game of stickball instead. When I arrived home, hot and exhausted, I found to my dismay that the coal man, unable to gain access to the chute and finding no one at home, had delivered the coal anyway. He had poured out a vast cone of shiny black coal onto the sidewalk.

As I looked at the massive and overwhelming pile, I realized that with my limited strength, it would take me hours to shovel it down the chute. How could I face my father? How could I explain my delinquency without confirming his poor opinion of my lackadaisical inability to follow simple instructions; my lack of responsibility; my foolishness; my time-wasting activities with my no-good friends; my this; my that. Oh, Papa would have a field day with his recriminations.

Just then Papa arrived, looked at the scene, and exclaimed, "How could I have forgotten?" He did not recall that he had assigned me the task of waiting for the coal man, and so he took the blame upon himself.

"How could I have forgotten?" he exclaimed. "I can't leave the coal here. It will get stolen and I'll get a ticket for littering and blocking the sidewalk. Here, you help me and we will shovel the coal down the chute ourselves."

Grateful to be off the hook, and without complaint, I hastened to open the chute, secured shovels, and, putting my eight-year-old shoulders to the task, helped Papa shovel the coal down the chute. I even hurried to get a large broom and swept the coal dust into the gutter. Papa was so grateful for my industry and willingness to work without murmuring, that he gave me the stupendous sum of one whole dollar.

That night, in the privacy of the bedroom, Papa told Mama, "The boy forgot to be there when the coal man arrived. But he looked so upset and so bewildered as he looked down at the pile of coal, I didn't have the heart to berate him. I think he learned a good lesson from it. Besides, he learned that there are times when the truth will only cause pain and there is a time for silence."

Version Two

As I looked at the massive pile of shiny black coal spilled out on the sidewalk, Papa arrived. He took the situation in at a glance.

"You forgot to be here when the coal man arrived!" he thundered. "So now you will have to shovel it down yourself!"

"But since it is partly my own fault for depending on you, I'll pay you a dollar for shoveling it in."

He handed over the dollar and left with a parting shot: "Have it done before supper, if you expect to eat."

The pile looked overwhelming. I could never get it done before supper! Just then two large boys from the local parochial school came by.

I approached them with an offer. "Would you guys shovel the coal down the chute for me and I'll pay you?"

"How much?" asked the larger.

"Fifty cents—each," I replied.

"Sixty," countered the boy.

"Okay," I replied. As they briskly and competently shoveled the coal, I went upstairs and secured the additional twenty cents from my hidden savings. The job was completed rather quickly and as I was paying off my "workers," Papa arrived.

"What is this?" he queried.

"They helped me out and I am paying them for it," I responded. The two employees hastily grabbed their money and left before Papa could change the arrangement.

"How much did you pay them?" he asked.

"Sixty cents each," I replied.

"But that is twenty cents more than you got from me. You lost money on the deal," said Papa.

"Well, for twenty cents it was worth it to be a boss."

That night, in the privacy of the bedroom, Papa said to Mama, "I liked the way he organized the job of the coal today. The boy is a born boss. He is a little foolish and he needs to learn something about costs and overhead and profit, but he is a natural supervisor and will be a good businessman some day."

VERSION THREE

The massive pile of shiny black coal on the sidewalk looked overwhelming. How could I cope with it? Papa arrived just then and took the situation in at a glance.

"You forgot to be here when the coal man arrived!" he thundered. "Now you will have to shovel it down yourself. Because it's partly my fault, I'll give you a dollar. Have it done before supper, if you expect to eat," he said at parting.

Just then two large boys from the local parochial school passed by and I approached them with an offer.

"Would you shovel the coal down the chute for me? I'll pay you."

"How much?" asked the larger.

"Fifty cents each," I responded.

"How do we know you have the dollar?" countered the larger.

Aghast that I should be accused of such chicanery, I pulled forth the dollar bill Papa had given me and waved it at them. "Here it is," I said proudly.

Whereupon the larger one punched me in the nose and the smaller one snatched the bill and both fled down the street, laughing happily.

Humiliated and in pain from my bloody nose, I now faced the task of shoveling the coal, without aid and without pay, and perhaps without supper. Angry and surly, I furiously attacked the coal, while cursing the coal man's ancestry and the ancestry of the thieves. I hurled the coal down the chute with a fury beyond my years and strength.

As I completed the task, including sweeping up, Papa arrived on the scene. It was obvious that he was pleased and somewhat astonished at the now-vanished coal pile.

"How did you do it so quickly?" he asked.

Unwilling to explain the motivation, I replied as children often do, "I just did."

"Well, that deserves another dollar," said Papa. "I'll match your dollar with another. What did you do with it?"

Unwilling to explain my naiveté and my humiliation, I made

matters worse.

"I spent it," I responded.

"You spent it? On what?"

"Candy and things," I replied.

"A whole dollar?" he asked with hurt astonishment.

"*Narishkeit* [foolishness]," he said and withdrew the offer of the matching dollar.

That night, in the privacy of the bedroom, Papa said to Mama, "I am disappointed in the boy. Not only does he forget to wait for the coal man, but he works like a horse for a dollar and then he spends it foolishly. He is irresponsible!" (The ultimate crime in a middle class home.)

"He can't be trusted with money. No matter how hard I try, he will never amount to anything."

"He is only a child, only eight," murmured Mama.

"Only a child?" said Papa, "When I was his age, I ..."

VERSION FOUR

As I looked at the massive pile of shiny black coal on the sidewalk, Papa arrived on the scene. He said...

The reader is free to write his or her own version of events.

Rope, Wheel and Pins

One sound that has always symbolized apartment life for me is a rasping squeal accompanied by a cold draft. It meant that Mama was leaning out of the window and working the clothes-line and the pulley-wheel was squeaking in protest.

Every apartment or flat, as we called it, was equipped with at least one of these outdoor dryers, and while it served the family, it was served in turn by the family's high priestess in charge of cleanliness. Each wheel, even the newest ones, seemed to come with a built-in shriek. One could even learn to recognize the distinctive squeal of one's own line among all of the other seemingly identical lines.

Fastened to the window frame with an enormous hook, the line stretched to a pole or to the opposite wall of what was jovially called the "courtyard." This was a narrow, sun-shunning space between buildings. The length of the line dictated the quantity of clothes one could hang out on it. However, too long a line became difficult to handle, especially loaded with plenty of damp *vesch* [wash]. The snapping of a line was an embarrassment and a catastrophe. It meant picking up your now soiled laundry under the mocking gaze of one's neighbors, as well as lengthy and costly negotiations with the super to have the line replaced.

In pre-dryer days, everyone washed and hung clothes out to dry almost daily. A large family provided the housewife with plenty of material to exercise her back over the *vash-braytel*, a corrugated metal knuckle buster. Then the damp clothes were wrung out by sheer muscle power. No wonder my mother could give us a *knip* [pinch] that could paralyze a horse. She had plenty of practice squeezing towels and pillowcases.

Getting a long wet sheet out on the line without letting it slap against the soiled building walls was a lesson in strength, timing and grace. Filling a line properly with the varied objects that made up the daily quota—socks, shirts, sheets, and so on—involved a knowledge of space, fabric and tensile strength worthy of a production engineer. Yet every day the courtyards were filled with loaded lines, gaily flapping pennants in the wind, as the women exposed the family laundry to public scrutiny and inventory, as well as to the sun.

One could tell a lot about a family from its display on the laundry lines. One could see the children growing up as diapers were replaced by bloomers and union suits. One could see the lengthening and shortening of garments as they were handed down to the next child in line. Even the family income could be estimated by the quality and number of the father's shirts on display. In a precarious economic life, where slack periods seemed to alternate only with strike periods, the number of *lottis* [patches] rose inversely with Papa's income.

The naïve may think that the clothes were draped over the line. Perish the thought! They were pinned there by means of a split wooden peg with a small head, which was used to pull the pin loose. None of these la-de-da spring type clothespins for us. You needed *koyech* [strength] to push them on and even more to remove these bifurcated tools.

God bless the man who invented the wooden clothespin, that wonderful toy of my youth. Not only could you show contempt for your friends by placing one jauntily on your nose to indicate that they smelled bad, but you could use them as an endless variety of make-believe toys. These sturdy, simple and cheap objects could be anything. They provoked us into wild flights off fancy in which these pins became men, cars, dragons, or locomotives, or they could be stuck together and provide us with World War I fighter plans, troops of cavalry, skyscrapers—anything we could imagine, they were. They fought, they marched, they soared, and we were the undisputed rulers of these fairy kingdoms until Mama said, "Enough already! Put back the clothes pins in the bag by the window."

On cold days the wet laundry would freeze and the whole family would help Mama haul the frosty crackling linen back into the house. Some of my more interesting nightmares stem from the sight of stiff, mummified long johns dancing weirdly in the watery January sunshine. A long rainy stretch meant that the bathroom, crowded already, had to serve as the drying room, and one would stoop and wriggle among the damp garments in order to use the facilities.

The laundry line, the clothespins, all are removed from the experience of our children and I would be committed if I suggested that we return to these primitive devices. But they did provide some values that are not present in the action of removing the lint from an electric clothes dryer. They gave the women a chance to *chop a bissel luft* [get some air] and schmooze with the "next doorkie" performing the same chore. The gaily flapping lines gave the neighborhood a spurious aspect of cheerful and colorful movement. It was as though they were the banners of an army filled with the hope that the next step would be to move out of the neighborhood to a community that had automatic dryers.

Miss Grey

In the section of Brooklyn called East New York, on Sutter Avenue, between Grafton and Legion Street, there exists a massive pile of red brick and limestone coping called Public School 156. It has been there a long, long time. It was there, about seventy years ago, that I endeavored to gain an education within the New York City public school system. It was an old building then. There I had the second turning in my life (I would have several more), and I write this to express my amazement and my gratitude that someone came to save me from myself.

To understand this you must know something about the protagonist. I was a bright but morose child, with a short temper and a wicked tongue. Throughout my early school career, my report card would bear the following designations: Work-A, Conduct-D. Since we received report cards each month, that meant that at least once a month my father gave me a beating. He would not listen to my explanations. To our immigrant minds, the teacher was an *Ubermensch* [superman] and always right. All the student had to do was to behave.

To confound the issue, there were two other factors. While I was a strong boy who was not bothered by minor childhood ailments, I would frequently come down with extremely serious illnesses, such as osteomyelitis (gangrene of the bone), scarlet fever, diphtheria and a torn stomach lining. So I spent some parts of each year between ages four and ten in various free public hospitals like Kings County. All I got out of those experiences was an affinity for bland, tasteless food, a dislike of condiments and salad dressings and a keen distrust of doctors and hospitals. Despite these episodes, I was able to keep up with my studies because I was an omnivorous reader.

I also was a traveling latchkey child. Since my mother worked side by side with my father in his kosher butcher shop, I was expected to come home, eat something and do my homework, unsupervised. Since we moved frequently to follow my father's different business locations, I would finish up the term by traveling to and from school via an assortment of trolleys and buses. This gave me a strong sense of independence and adventure. I got to know many of the drivers on the various transit vehicles and they would often close an eye when I neglected to pay the five-cent fare. That money would immediately be applied to the price of a second-hand book like Tom Swift or the Boy Allies or some Civil War trash by Atherton. (I never bought a new book until I went to college.) I also consumed pulp magazines like *Argosy, Blue Book* and any Hugo Gernsback science-fiction magazine like *Amazing Stories.*

My most treasured possession was my public library borrower's card. Since one was only allowed to borrow two books at a time, a date stamp mounted on the end of a pencil duly noting the due date on your card, I would soon use up my card. It was during this period that I encountered and fell in love with the junk written by Rafael Sabatini, who wrote sea and historical costume novels like *Captain Blood* and *Scaramouche.* Eventually I read almost every one of his 23 novels before the romance wore off.

During the summer, without schoolwork, I could devote myself to virtually full-time reading. Every other day I would trudge to the large stone library on Eastern Parkway, about a mile walk each way, and park my chewing gum under the iron rail before I entered. The librarian was amazed.

"Do you really read all these or are you showing off?"

I was hurt.

"Ask me about any part of them," I challenged. We became friends and I have loved all librarians and all people connected with books and print since.

So we have a bright, articulate and well-read youngster trapped in a classroom that operated on the convoy system. That is, the teacher set the pace to accommodate the slower children to keep them from falling behind. There were no homogeneous classes (except the "two" class which was the "dumb" class). So, long after I had gotten the idea, sometimes before the teacher had completed her first sentence, the teacher was painfully going over and over and over the same worn pedestrian idea until I became frantic and restless. A restless child soon gets into mischief and I did. Whispering, playing games, reading my own books behind the big geography text, I would incur the wrath of the teacher. Sometimes to speed up the learning process, I would call out answers and mutter loudly about stupid people. This did not create much good will towards me in the classroom, so there were many who were delighted to inform the teacher that "Milton was not doing his assignment." Years later, when I was a teacher, any snitch got short shrift from me.

Some teachers tried to cow me with their knowledge. That usually failed because I held most of them in low esteem since I had learned that in some areas, such as geography, history and trashy literature, I knew as much as they. Besides, I discovered that when one did not know a fact one could make it up and convince the teacher that one was smart.

I also had the unfortunate habit of being quick with my tongue and could reduce the class (but not the teacher) to gales of laughter. That resulted in frequently whacked knuckles. Most of my Irish and Yankee teachers were quite adept at swinging a ruler or yardstick and did so without any guilt feelings. I also "enjoyed" frequent trips to the principal's office for punishment.

One teacher decided to lock me into the wardrobe closet, a broad, shallow crypt filled with damp, smelly outer garments. I was so enraged at the humiliation that using a small penknife, I cut the left sleeve (I don't know why the left only) off several garments that were staring me in the face. That caused an uproar equal to the announcement of Armistice Day.

My father came to school, thereby losing time away from his precious store, and agreed to compensate all of the aggrieved parents, and then took me home for my beating. I had become fairly adept at dodging his roundhouse swings, but this time I dodged the wrong way and slammed into a bone-cutting blade, deeply cutting my right upper lip. So we all went to the hospital for stitching and further recriminations. I still carry the scar (the real reason I wore a mustache and now a beard).

After that episode, which gave me wide notoriety, teachers coped with me by sending me out of the room. I became editor of the grade newspaper and a permanent messenger or monitor delivering messages and books and cleaning blackboards. I did not mind. I would drop into my class briefly and keep up with the rest of the students with ease. It gave me a broader world view. I would visit the classrooms of my siblings, wash the blackboards and hear them proudly announce to their classmates, "That's my brother." I learned a bit about school administration that stood me in good stead many years later.

The day established for what was jovially called Assembly was a special day in the N.Y.C. public schools. Everyone, no matter from how poor or disorganized a household, was expected to come to school with a sparkling white shirt and a red, sometimes blue, knitted tie (the girls wore middy blouses with red or blue scarves). How neat and disciplined everyone looked. We were expected to be on our best behavior as we listened to the Holy Writ as expounded by the principal.

As we lustily sang the "Star Spangled Banner," I decided to playfully pull the shirt out of the belt of the singer in front of me, He angrily turned around to strike me, but I beat him to the punch. The teacher was horrified at the disturbance, as it reflected on her as the keeper of discipline, and the principal ordered me to his office. There he announced that I must bring my father and mother to school or I would be suspended and expelled from school.

I was in a quandary. To tell my father, so soon after the other contretemps, would bring instant annihilation. Not to tell him would ruin my hopefully promising career. So, I did nothing. Several days passed without anything happening while I hunkered down in my classroom, so I supposed that all had been forgotten. Little did my childish mind know of files and reminders. The summons from on high to report to the principal's office came, delivered by a delighted teacher anxious to see me punished.

"Why haven't your parents come?" queried the principal. He was unique in that he was Jewish, in an environment that in those days was still heavily weighted towards Irish and WASP personnel. My gift for fiction came to my rescue. I tearfully delineated a tale of deep sorrow. My mother was quite ill, my father's business was on the verge of bankruptcy and my sister was in the hospital. It was a soap opera long before the term was created and not bad for a fifth grader.

The principal was touched and I could see that he was moved to refrain from adding to the overwhelming load on this unfortunate family. "Is this true?" he asked.

His face was so trusting and vulnerable that I could not resist saying, "Not a word of it."

His face contorted with shock, then he burst into laughter. *"Verdray dir dein kopf* [Drive yourself crazy]," he said and chased me out of his office. I never heard about the matter again, but I did gain a lot of respect for the principal's good sense. Many years later, at a professional association meeting, he told me he thought I was bright but completely insane. Who was I to tell him he was wrong? Besides it was pleasant to know that people remembered me.

The following year, in sixth grade, while I was slightly chastened, my behavior pattern did not vary very much. My parents had moved to Borough Park, where my father had established a new store, but I was finishing out the year at the same school. The reason that I did not move was that I had taken the exam for Rapid Advance classes, a new program that would permit me to finish the three years in junior high school in two.

The R.A. classes were an innovation which assembled the brightest students (those with over 130 I.Q.) in one class and subjected them to a more rapid coverage of the schoolwork, hence the name. I knew that I wanted to be in one of those classes and moving away in mid-year would mean the loss of a significant opportunity.

But I still continued to be one of the terrors of the school to the teachers, though not to the other students. I was never a bully or a menace, just a pain in the neck to the rigid staff.

One day after some escapade, I was racing down the hallway to avoid being caught, when a teacher stepped into the hallway to determine the cause of the commotion. Bam! With my head down, and unable to stop in time, I struck her amidships like a battering ram. She went down and her pince-nez glasses went flying the other way. I glanced down in terror and continued my flight. Boy, was I in trouble now! I hastily found my home-room and settled down, hoping my victim had not gotten a good look at me. Perhaps, with 2,000 pupils in the school, she might not know me.

Just before the dismissal at the end of the day, she appeared at the door of my room: Miss Grey. I knew her as one of the coldest spinsters in the school, though almost all of the teachers, except the few Jewish ones, were spinsters. She spoke quietly to my teacher who said to me, "Go with Miss Grey." I rose with fear. Only the greater fear of looking like a coward to my classmates caused me to walk out quietly, without quivering.

I walked behind Miss Grey, clothed in a gray, silk dress, wear-ing her schoolmarm watch on her slightly sagging bosom, fair hair in a bun, head erect, peering at the world fiercely through her now recovered pince-nez glasses. She had never been one of my teachers, but the school scuttlebutt was that she was a real taskmaster and not one to be trifled with. We walked to her now empty room where she ordered me to sit in one of the student seats.

I knew this was no time for my strident sense of humor, but she shocked me when she asked, "Were you hurt?"

"No," I said, "Were you?"

Neither of us made any pretense about incorrect identifica-tion. We both knew I was the culprit and we were not bother-ing with preliminary fencing.

"Slightly," she said, "but it was my fault. I should have dodged you. For a boy who recently took off his braces you run quite well."

How did she know about me? None of my other teachers ever referred to my absences or my various handicaps. She actually smiled at me! I apologized for running into her and promised never to do it again. She accepted the apology with grace and then continued the conversation.

"Why are you such a nuisance? I have watched you for a few terms. You know, you are a frequent topic of conversation in the upper grade teacher's lounge."

I didn't even know that teachers ate or used the bathroom, much less that they talked about students like me.

"Everyone thinks you are incorrigible. Most can't wait until you leave and I can't blame them. You have a fine mind and a splendid vocabulary. I love the grade newspaper you publish every month. Where did you get the name 'News-Caster'?"

"I put together the words 'Newspaper' and 'Broadcasting.'"

"Very original. Do you write most of the material yourself?"

"Most, especially the fake poems and the funny stories. The other kids write about events in the school that are too boring for me."

"Why do you call them fake poems?"

"Well, I copy old poems like "The Ride of Paul Revere" and then I make up different words for them that sound similar but come out much funnier."

"Those are called parodies," she said.

I carefully stored that word for future reference.

The conversation continued long after the school grew quiet. Nothing is as quiet as a school after the children and staff have left. No teacher had ever spoken to me as though

I were a person before. Until then I had been an object to be ordered and coerced. She made no attempt to tone down her vocabulary in view of my tender years, nor did she need to. This was the first conversation with an adult that I had enjoyed. Despite my parents' overwhelming love of me, they never really talked to me or listened to me. Their conversation consisted of endearments, warnings, admonitions, pronouncements and queries about fever, appetite and bowel movements.

When I realized how time had passed, I said I must go home because my parents would be worried sick. When she learned that I had more than an hour trip via two buses, she suggested that I travel with her in a taxi. I immediately agreed because it would save time and I could apply the nickel to my book fund. Besides, a taxi ride was such an unusual event in my life. We were great walkers in my family and a taxi fare seemed a ridiculous waste of hard-earned money.

In the cab, Miss Grey announced that since she traveled by my home every day in her taxi, it would be no trouble for her to take me along each day. And that was the way it was resolved. For the remaining months of the school year, I would meet Miss Grey in front of the school and we would travel in style to my home block, where she would drop me off with a grave, "Good afternoon."

At the time, I thought she was ancient, but on looking back she must have been about 35, but with the sadness and quiet despair one associates with the truly unhappy. Miss Grey might have longed to be married, but until only a few years earlier the Board of Education fired any teacher who married. So a career choice meant celibacy and non-marriage. (Incidentally, it was one of the first Jewish teachers hired who fought that restriction in court and won thereby breaking the rule of teacher-spinster that had persisted so long.)

While I had never heard of the word sublimation, I realized that she was venting some of her pain and loss by adopting a stray like me. She would use the time in the cab as an extra educational period, discussing books, plays, arts and philosophy, most of which went over my head. But it alerted me to an important concept; there was a large and mysterious world out there that was far different from the day-to-day struggles of life in Brownsville.

One day she asked me a curious question. "How much do you pay to be funny?"

I told her that I did not understand the question.

"Well, you are quick to tell jokes, usually to the annoyance of the teacher. While the class enjoys itself and howls, the teacher then takes it out on you and punishes you. You really don't like most of your classmates, yet you persist in playing the class clown, giving them pleasure, yet paying the price for all of the fun."

I was startled by the concept. Not that I was the class clown, as I had been called that before, but that I was the only one paying the piper. I resolved that henceforth I would restrain myself and limit my unorthodox comments to the printed page. I would not pay for everyone's fun to the detriment of my career.

I wish I could say that I managed to keep that resolve. I know that in the junior and senior high schools and in my checkered career, I often slipped. But on the whole I showed reasonable restraint. Miss Grey had turned me around to the point where I stopped being a *vilde chaya* [wild animal] and became a mere annoyance to the teachers. I also discovered that, over the reluctance of the principal and the protests of her colleagues, she had persisted and obtained for me one of the few and cherished admissions to the R.A. classes.

So the term ended and I left the school to move on to the brave new world of the Rapid Advance classes of the junior high. I was happier there and did quite well, despite the high caliber of competition. My family moved to the Bronx, but my admission to the R.A. was transferable.

Many years later, a colleague, then the principal of P.S. 156, unearthed my old record cards and we all had a good laugh about the boy with the A in Work and D in Conduct. A series of different teachers had all commented about me in these records. These could be summarized as, "An impossible child who never can keep his mouth shut and does not show any respect for his teachers."

Perhaps I became a principal and superintendent so as to get my revenge on those who I felt had tormented and underestimated me. Probably not. But I know that I became a teacher, and loved being a teacher, because of Miss Grey. I never saw her again, never contacted her or looked for her.

Her image remains with me: clear, quiet and luminous, tall, with a scrubbed clean look, ramrod erect, except for her head slightly tilted, like all good teachers, as she listened carefully to my ideas.

It is ironic that a woman from such a different background saw something in the boy who would some day become a school administrator. Quietly, without moralizing or lecturing, she taught him a powerful lesson that shaped his life. If I could talk to her, I'd say, God bless you, Miss Grey. Thank you, for showing me some respect and for saving my life. I'm sorry I took so long to get around to thanking you.

Crime in the Schools

All this furor that fills the news media about crime and violence in the schools is not a new phenomenon. We had lots of crime in the schools when I was a pupil. So I have listed the common forms of crime, infractions and misbehavior that prevailed when I was an elementary and high school student. (The crimes are not listed in order of severity.)

Whispering in class

Forgetting to bring in your homework

Coming to school without a handkerchief or a pencil

Being absent or late without a note from your parents

Peeking at a friend's test paper

Calling out an answer without raising your hand

Pushing in line or not standing in "size place"

Failing to stand when reciting

Not dressing properly for assembly day

Playing hooky or cutting class

Passing notes in class

Submitting homework copied from a friend

Ignoring the rule to "sit up tall"

Failing to say, in unison, "Good morning, teacher"

Coming to school without a tie or a middy blouse

Engaging in horseplay in the school yard

Getting into line out of turn when playing double dutch jump rope

Hanging your clothes in the wardrobe on the wrong hook

Returning textbooks in shabby condition

Submitting school work that wasn't neat

Throwing spitballs or erasers

Dipping your neighbor's long curls into the inkwell

For these and other innumerable serious high crimes and misdemeanors, the whole weight of the state descended upon the malefactor. The teachers, most of whom were Irish Catholic spinsters trying to teach Jewish boys and girls to be WASP ladies and gentlemen, felt free to deride the criminal, to push him into line, pull his ears, even whack him with a ruler or yardstick, without malice or guilt. No pupil dared to object, much less to answer back.

Notes were sent home to parents who, overcome by shame, immediately resolved the conflict by the liberal use of papa's strap.

Visits to the chamber of horrors, the principal's office, often followed. Sometimes the perpetrator was suspended, or left back, and the whole family went into mourning. The least sentence was always a reduced grade or a D in conduct on the monthly report card.

Those were terrible days for the teachers who had to suffer teaching such a wild and criminal element. They served as the thin red line between order and chaos.

The Two Shul President

Although he would furiously deny it when I mentioned it, Papa was not such a synagogue goer when he was younger. He worked seven days a week, including Saturday after sundown. (Saturday was the Sabbath and ended at sundown.) Saturday morning, when his kosher meat store was closed, was the only time he could rest from his strenuous labors. He faithfully attended *shul* [synagogue] on all holidays, and my brother and I were also expected to attend. We never said no until we reached the age of military service.

Another reason he did not attend services frequently was that he had a healthy skepticism, actually a distrust, of the organized clergy and the overly pious. I suspect that with his Germanic and military background he also looked down on the *Ostjuden* [Eastern European Jews] because they seemed so noisy and unkempt, in his opinion. It was only later, when he was involved in real estate and in the oil business, that he became much more active in synagogue affairs.

After his first heart attack, Papa discontinued his active life as a meat dealer and bought, managed and sold large apartment houses all over the Bronx. He also found time to become president of a Romanian relief organization to help Jews in Displaced Person camps, as well as the president of the local shul on East 174th Street and Longfellow Avenue.

It was a small shul, but not small enough to be called a *shtibel* [storefront] shul, with about 200 seats and a catering hall in the cellar for weddings and bar mitzvahs. It was a place of worship without pretensions. The old timers came there every morning for the *minyan* [quorum], put on *tefillin* [small boxes containing portions of scripture] and *shuckled* [swayed] or carried on private conversations while the Torah portion was read.

My everlasting impression was that it was always crowded and suffocatingly hot every holiday. We all sweltered in our new heavy woolen winter suits in the Indian summer weather of the High Holidays. Since the idea of a year-round membership fee had not yet taken hold, the synagogues would sell tickets for High Holiday attendance to sustain themselves and pay the rabbi. To prevent people who had not paid from sneaking in, they hired a security guard, usually some elderly gentleman who couldn't keep anyone out.

To increase income, they would also auction off the High Holiday *aliyot* [honors] on the *bimah* [dais], which occurred at significant points of the service. Some honors were considered more prestigious and therefore more valuable than others. I can recall the singsong calls of the *shammes* [sexton] as he dealt with the spirited bidding. "*Funf tooler fir shlishi dem ersten mool!*" [Five dollars for the third honor going once.] When the bidding went as far as it could, the sexton would called out the warning, "*Dem letzen mool*" [the last time], and the last bidder would be awarded the honor. Since no one was permitted to carry money on the holidays, it was on the honor system, and you would redeem your pledge as soon as possible. Woe to the person who reneged! It was a real *shande* [scandal].

Papa would not deign to enter this auction, because he thought the whole process was demeaning. He would sit quietly until a major honor was up for bid and then he would nod to the shammes, who would call out, "*Mr. Stier git finf und zwan-zig tooler*" [gives 25 dollars] and that sum, usually greater than any bid anticipated, would stifle all other bids. Occasionally, some newcomer, unaware of who Mr. Stier was, would bid higher and find that the shammes ignored his bid.

After we moved to Longfellow Avenue, he joined the synagogue and soon rose to a position of prestige. He was the perpetual president of the synagogue and he ruled it with a firm hand.

Papa selected the rabbi and the cantor, when the need arose, and discharged them when he felt the need. He also had a hand in selecting all of the board members and heads of the various committees of the synagogue. He also tried, but failed, to get them to discontinue the aliyot auction, but he succeeded in establishing annual membership dues and eliminating the demeaning tickets.

Papa was hard working, efficient and scrupulously honest. When he delegated authority, the task was promptly carried out. Most of the members liked the strong leadership. But some became quite restive under his dictatorship. So, as it happens in many congregations, a group splintered off and decided to set up their own, non-Stier, synagogue.

They purchased a building on the same block and opened it in competition with the old synagogue. Unfortunately, the same inability to work with strong leaders that had caused the break also made it impossible for them to select a board or a president.

After months of wrangling and squabbling, without a rabbi or a leader but unwilling to return to the fold in shame, they approached my father to help them out. Would he please serve as the "temporary" president until the new synagogue leadership could take over?

Papa gravely considered the plan—and agreed! What was remarkable to me is that he saw nothing remarkable or incongruous about it. He felt he was only being given the respect he deserved.

And so he served as the president of the new shul, where he selected the rabbi and the cantor, and as the president of the old shul, going to each on alternate Sabbaths. This unique arrangement continued for about two years until the new synagogue closed and, with honor and pride intact, all of the dissident group returned to the original house of worship, with Joe Stier still president.

I recall one day Papa got a lot of *naches* [joy] from me in that shul. It was my first Sabbath back from overseas army duty and I still wore my full uniform, medals and all. In those days I weighed a lean, tough 165 pounds and was not bad looking. I was given an important aliyah to honor my safe return. Papa proudly shared the bimah with me on that occasion.

I was then asked to say a few words. I didn't know what I should say. I know that I could have recited "Mary Had a Little Lamb" and gotten overwhelming applause. A Jewish soldier, a healthy and hardened veteran, was a sight these elderly, passive Jews loved. I don't know why, but I launched into a tale of my visit to Dachau, all in Yiddish, and the audience grew silent. I closed with expressions of gratitude for coming home to America, safe and well. When I finished, the deathly silence continued, then most of them burst into tears and applause and pushed their way up to the bimah to touch me, to shake my hand, and to praise me. Papa smiled quietly, but his pride showed through.

The neighborhood eventually changed and the membership of the 174th Street shul dwindled to virtually nothing. Papa, still a dues-paying member, was living some distance away, near the Moshulu Parkway Jewish Center, where he was, of course, the president. He was asked by the small membership of the synagogue, who still remembered him fondly, to help them out. He reviewed their options and suggested that the synagogue be closed and all of them shift to another nearby shul. They agreed, and he sold the building to a Puerto Rican church group, who still run an Iglesia there. He contributed the sale price of $35,000 to the United Jewish Appeal.

Years later, the Internal Revenue Service, suspecting that my father had absconded with the funds, investigated the sale. His lawyer, now a well-known law professor and jurist, came to the rescue. My father had been his first client and they had developed a life-long friendship, even though Papa still called him "Daniel" and he still called Papa "Mr. Stier."

Papa spoke in his own defense. Even though the government claimed that Papa had no right to arbitrarily dispose of the money by giving it away, there was no evidence of dishonesty. Papa was, as usual, squeaky clean, and the matter was dropped. After all, could a man who was the president of two shuls be dishonest?

The Forgotten City

It was customary for successful young men to come back to the Bronx community in which I was raised to visit their mothers. This gave rise to a warm sharing of pleasure and *naches* [joy] as the mother introduced the success to her *bekannter* [acquaintances] and each would loudly asset that they always knew he would make something of himself. They had recognized great promise in the noisy stickball player whom they had roundly berated years ago. But now he was a professional man, or a small businessman, or working in the civil service, and everyone rejoiced in the shared memory and reflected glory.

My memories, my opportunity to bask in the glory of the neighbors' admiration, in my mother's *farginigen* [pleasure] as she proudly stroked my cheek while reciting my accomplishments, some imaginary, but all inflated, to her chorus of admiring friends—all this has been stolen from me. The Bronx, especially the east Bronx where I was raised, has been obliterated. There is no one there who remembers me, or the millions like me. There is no chorus of friends, no second generation ringo-leavio players, no one to whom I would be of interest—so I have been robbed, impoverished without enriching anyone else.

Just as we mourn the passing of the Six Million and the way of life they practiced, we also mourn the communities and social fabric of the *shtetl* [ghetto], the *Talmud Torahs* [religious school for boys], the *Kehilla* [communal organization], the intricate institutions that made for a way of life now gone, fallen, like the people, into the silent well of history.

For about 50 years, from approximately 1910, when the new subway lines opened up tracts of land on which to construct vast apartment buildings, to about 1960, when the community tipped into minority-group occupancy, a *Yiddishe medina* [Jewish community] flourished in most of the Bronx.

Jewish institutions, transplanted from the lower East Side, grew into a network of synagogues, societies, and "egg-si-la-ries" (auxiliaries); a network of ZOA [Zionist Organization of America] and UJA [United Jewish Appeal]; of HIAS [Hebrew Immigrant Aid Society] and B'Nai B'rith; all of which tied together the flourishing and expanding community. Along the strivers' row called the Grand Concourse sprang up magnificent apartment houses and synagogues, concrete testaments to the growing economic success of the Bronx Jews in the professions, the business world and the civil service. The upwardly mobile retailer was shaping the community into his own image.

Even in the East Bronx, on Tinton Avenue and Longfellow Avenue, on Minford Place, on Jenning Street and Kelly Street, the desire to build, though on a less grandiose scale, produced its own series of prideful projects. Oh, how the building funds grew and how the committees strove to reach and surpass their goals. How many "bricks" (contributions to the building funds) were sold!

By the mid-thirties, despite the fierce Depression, the social fabric which held the community together was established and in place. The Bronx appeared to me like one vast shtetl in which almost everyone was Jewish. On the High Holy Days the entire borough shut down as virtually every retailer, druggist and dentist walked to *shul* [synagogue] with his *tallith* [prayer shawl].

I can recall one Yom Kippur morning when the silent streets in front of my father's shul were marred by a group of sanitation men deliberately banging the garbage cans. The younger men of the congregation sallied forther to drive the yahoos away. Despite the *shande* [scandal] involved in the desecration of the holy day, I noted my father's glance of approval when he saw my bloody nose. The Jews were *davening* [praying] and the *goyim* [non-Jews] were to respect that holy day.

Where is the bustle, the noise, the sheer greed and electric vitality of the pushcart market of Bathgate Avenue? The *bale-batesha* [bourgeois] shopkeepers of Tremont Avenue? Gone, gone, to be replaced by fast-food chains and fortune tellers. The streets, as I write this, are faced with rapidly decaying and destroyed apartment buildings, and filled with broken glass and dog excrement. The buildings, where they still exist, are hollow-eyed, bombed-out shells—havens only for junkies and rats. The kosher butcher has fled with his customers, and the signs in Hebrew hang mockingly over empty stores.

The rabbi and the *chazzan* [cantor] have followed their flocks to the suburbs and the shuls are empty. Some have become black churches or Hispanic Iglesias, but most are empty, waiting—waiting for what? Waiting for those who have gone to seek peace in other places, in Scarsdale and Great Neck, in Roslyn and Rockland County? And the synagogues remain, waiting and waiting—and dead?

Where is the *minyan* [quorum]? Who looks at the bronze memorial plaques on the walls, once cherished and loved, but now forgotten? Perpetual care has lasted all of one generation. The *chupeh* [bridal canopy] which echoed to the sound of the broken glass hangs limp. The caterer has removed his equipment and the stoves are as cold as the winter wind. The echo of the hearty *Mazel Tov* [congratulations] and the chant of the anguished chazzan are still. Gone are the *aliyahs* [honors in the service], the breakfasts, the dances, the ponderous installations and the endless minutes of the last meeting. Who walks where the sisterhood once engaged in furious debate on the nature of the adult program? Who cares if you hade the title of Past President or whether you gave a golden page in the Journal?

The shell is there, but the spirit of the house of God, the *olim* [people], is gone. The *Sefar Torahs* [Torah scrolls] now grace the ark of some shining new structure on Long Island. The teachers and students are gone, but the *bimahs* [daises] stand empty, waiting the tread of the worshippers… but none appear. The outmoded shuls have been replaced by elegant architectural triumphs in Woodmere and East Meadow.

The shuls have been left behind, victims of prosperity and change. Should we preserve them? Do they qualify as historic monuments? Do they earn some respect because of the burning passion, the pride, the vanity, the faith in the future that caused them to be built? Should they be preserved because of the great occasions they housed—the somber *yiskors* [memorial prayers]; the bray of the *shofar* [ram's horn]; the floor-thumping jolts of the hora; the exaltation of the final *N'eela* [closing service of Yom Kippur]? Yet nothing seems to remain.

The walls do not echo back the impassioned sermons; the bagels and lox are gone and not a crumb or aroma remain. How the davening droned and thundered and how spirited the bidding for the aliyahs—"*Zwei tooler far shlishi dem dritten mool!*" [Two dollars for the third honor going for the third time.] Here the smelling salts were passed during services, disdained and ostentatiously ignored by the stronger worshippers; here was a sense of awe as the righteous prostrated themselves before the ark. But none of this can be seen through the cracked stained glass windows. Vandals have been here and will return.

Who recalls Mr. Blanks' commitment, fierce and loud, to traditional education? Who remembers the golden tones of Chazzan Aleph in the shul on Kelly Street? Or the plaques awarded to Mrs. Gimmel for her strenuous activities in the service of the sisterhood? The cries of "I second the motion," the debates in executive meetings over budgets, all the awkward machinery needed to keep the Eternal Light going, it is all now stilled. Is temple dust holier than other dust? Does the shell of the House of the Lord deserve any veneration when the spirit—the people—have been removed?

Do the carpet runners up the main aisle still preserve the tread of the *kahle* [bride], the bouncing stride of the Simchas Torah procession; the shuffle of the Bar Mitzvah *bucher* [student]? Or is it just a damp, faded and mildewed layer of the wool? Do the pews, hard and unyielding, still remember how everyone swayed as "Ah Nachnu Koreem" sounded? Is it just another empty structure, cast away by the community, just another abandoned building waiting for the strippers and the torch of vandalism?

And just as the bustling *yiddishkeit* [Jewish culture] of the living community has departed, so have the cities of the dead, the cemeteries of our community, also been abandoned. What is a cemetery when no one comes? A grave? No, a marbled wasteland bewailing its loss to the unheeding sky.

When the Jews became numerous in a city, they immediately established cemeteries and each man bought his plot, sometimes as an individual, but more likely through a society or lodge.

They bought final resting places in Montefiore, in Hebron, in Mt. Judah and Zion, so that the terrible contingency of not having a "place" could be avoided. They bought family plots, some with space for grandchildren. They provided for a future that might never come, because the potential residents of these extra spaces no longer live in the area. The olim are gone.

Even the older generation has gone to sit in the sunny *Gan Eden* [garden of Eden] of Miami, only returning for the funerals of their loved ones, counting their loss and bewailing the passings—then dispersing to La Jolla, Atlanta, and Northport, not to return to the cemetery until another funeral or headstone unveiling, when, like actors, they appear again on the scene. Who can visit between funerals when the trip is so inconvenient? Who needs to visit when memory, buttressed by photographs in living color, keep the name fresh?

So, as we move on to the prosperous suburbs, we leave behind our aged and our dead. And the cemeteries become not a blessing and a remembrance, but a place of the truly dead: the forgotten.

As one looks at the unvisited cemetery, one is struck by the contrast with the grave of the RamBam, Moses Maimonedes, which has been visited and been the scene of much prayer for a millennium. Why? Because the people who remember him still feel connected, and therefore the grave is alive, even though he is a memory from the far past.

I wonder whether I should elect to take the place purchased for me by my father in the family plot. Although I visit his grave because I still live in the area, will my children do the same for me? They already live hundreds of miles away, and who knows where they will end their days. It will no doubt be inconvenient for them to visit. As for my grandchildren, who knows what funeral arrangements will be customary when they reach the age of worrying about plots. So who will pause? Who will perch little pebbles on the shoulder of my headstone? There is a place for me, but should I take it?

Do I want to lie among the silent array of granite… unvisited? Even more than the vandals that upset stones and steal bronze doors, the ultimate desecrators are the non-visitors, those who do not appear because they have followed their star to other places. The brief stay of the Yiddishe Medina, the bustling vital community of the Bronx, is marked only by the concrete desert of wrecked buildings and grave monuments staring blank-eyed, like the status of Easter Island, waiting for those who will not appear.

Out in the World

A Young Man in the '30s

There were few, if any, books in my home on Longfellow Avenue. Talk was limited to the bare essentials of life: business matters, family, health and the latest horror in the daily *Forvert*, a Yiddish newspaper. (My mother was fascinated by strikes and accidents, and I recall her eagerly and anxiously reading aloud the full details about the famous shipwreck of the Vestria and the great loss of life.) As a result, I was a Columbus on a sea of ignorance about literature and culture. All I learned about these significant areas was from a few friends, especially female friends. They taught me about music, ballet and art. I was a sponge about these matters, but hampered by my poor memory.

Anxious to appear polished, I would pretend to far more knowledge and sophistication than I had. I was always afraid of revealing my ignorance about some simple matter. And I was always being caught out because I did not know about many things, such as the Cloisters or New York's many art museums or Lewisohn Stadium, where you sat high on concrete seats and listened to divine music under the open night sky. But I learned. Despite working long hours in the store and going to school at night, I still found time to read and visit cultural sites.

I recall what a revelation it was to see *The Bartered Bride* at the Lewisohn or to go to Madison Square Garden—for the horse show, no less. I was the only young man of my milieu who rode horses. I actually owned one, named Cheyenne, that I kept boarded at a riding academy on Pelham Parkway.

I was immature, yet I seemed to act maturely. At least, people treated me that way—except my women. They always knew I was really a kid, and a frightened one at that.

I was a pretender. I pretended to have more knowledge, more courage and more sophistication than I had. I pretended to have greater ambitions and greater talents. I tended to be flamboyant in speech and dress, simply because I did not like what I was. I was in a perpetual state of anxious dissatisfaction. I told tall tales and outright lies about myself, my career, my family background—once I even concocted the tale that I was a German baron! Sometimes I resorted to mysterious hints about my unusual, and possibly lurid, background to enhance my image and my possible attraction to women. Most of my male friends detested me for this and I wasn't particularly successful with the girls, either. Since my memory was poor, I found it difficult to keep these lies straight and to remember which story I had told to which person. When I was found out, I was surprised that others were upset. Didn't everyone stretch the truth about themselves?

Sex was a major topic of my youth. Not that we practiced it, but we talked about it all the time. I suspect we were in a constant state of sexual tension and it colored our thoughts, our talk and our dreams. Girls were pursued for their favors and we eagerly sought those who would "put out." I heard many stories and many brags, but there was very little fire for all of that smoke.

No matter how we talked about sex amongst ourselves, we were careful never to use dirty language in front of our girls or our parents. We didn't feel that we had the right to use dirty words, even when describing dirty people or dirty events. Rough workers, like teamsters, butchers, and mechanics, were forgiven for using the word "fuck," because they were "common" anyway. We had to watch ourselves, especially in our white-collar work places.

At the work place, we followed the rules. The dress code was iron-bound. Men were expected to wear a white shirt, a neat tie, and a somber, conservative suit, of grey, blue or brown, with everything matching and clean. A man without blindingly polished shoes was considered a bum. Back then you could buy a cheap suit for $18 and a fine English overcoat for $50. Wingtip shoes were popular and also Monk shoes, a shoe fastened at the instep with a broad strap with the buckle towards the outer side.

Girls, almost all secretaries or teachers, wore neat blouses and suits in restrained colors. They wore gloves and hats whenever leaving the house, especially on a date.

Most of us took the subway to work and we always felt safe and comfortable. The trains were crowded during the rush hours, yet everyone seemed clean and self-contained as they went to work. No one bothered anyone else. People did not smoke or spit, and vandalism, except in very rare instances, was not a factor.

We expected the subways to run in any sort of weather They were the vital arteries of the city and were rarely blocked. One could travel from one end of the city to another for five cents, with no fear of crime. I recall taking a girl home to Brighton Beach late one night and riding back to the Bronx, all alone and asleep, with no fear except that I might ride pass my stop.

For entertainment, we went to the movies. Like all of my contemporaries, I was in love with movies, and the studios produced a Niagara of films every year. One could wander through the forest of films every day without seeing the same film twice. With the star system, we became familiar with the leading actors and would rush to see the new Leslie Howard or Spencer Tracey movie, no matter what the theme was. Sometimes free dishes were given away at the movies or there was a Bank Night, a sort of lottery based on the number on your ticket stub. But even if there wasn't such an event, everyone, except my parents, went at least once a week

I used to hang around with a group of friends on the corner of 174th Street. But for some reason, I was never as close to them as they were to each other, perhaps because I went to college and they did not. I would spend my time in the library while they went to New Jersey to see the burlesque. I often thought of them as loud, vulgar and given to coarse language and joking. Farting and belching were greeted with loud hilarity. They enjoyed such behavior and my obvious distaste for it did not endear me to them. They suspected that I had other interests, that there were other dimensions to my life, and I was drifting away from them.

Yet they were good sincere people, even though they were shallow. They could be very funny and we had happy times. They meant well and would give you the shirt off their backs. I don't remember ever going out on a double date with any of them. I must have kept my several lives compartmentalized. Some died in the war. I regret that I never really made any attempt to renew my friendship with the others after the war. I suspect that by then I had outgrown them, or they had drifted away from me. Perhaps I was just a snob. I should have realized that someone is a friend not only because you share the same interests, but because you care about one another. Sometimes the faces of the many friends I dropped come back to haunt me and I feel guilty.

For all of us, the war was the vast watershed that divided one's life. Looking back, I am surprised that in 1938 and 1939, with the war obviously on the way, I was so oblivious to the massing of the war clouds. It was a form of schizophrenia, going out with girls and reading books without any fear, while Kristalnacht took place. I was interested in my horse, my camera, my schoolwork, my job and my dates. The World's Fair of 1939 took precedence, in my mind, over these distant matters. When I went into Dachau as the war was drawing to a close and became fully aware of the gruesome details of the Final Solution, I was, and still remain, smitten with guilt over my indifference and my lack of action as Hitler rose to power.

I don't recall ever discussing Hitler or the persecution of the Jews with my friends. Except at some meetings of the Young Communists, where I was taken by a girl I was interested in, I never even though of these matters. As for the young radicals, I found their endless and fruitless discussions and hairsplitting dialectics a total bore. What frightened me was that they seemed so deadly serious about this intricate nonsense. They were prepared to kill to protect the party line. I never joined nor did I participate in their numerous boycotts and demonstrations. The Socialists, who were just as verbose, worshipped the ever-losing Norman Thomas. While he was a very decent person, he was a political *nebbish* [simpleton] who had his feet firmly planted in mid-air.

Most of the left-wingers, Communists and Socialists were Jews who proudly announced their lack of religion and *Yiddishkeit* [Jewish culture], but they acted like priests with a new religion—Marxism—and with the same blind fervor.

Worst of all, they were so everlastingly dull and self-righteous. Only they had the key to the kingdom of the future. What a slap in the mouth when their God, Stalin, kissed Hitler's ass with the Soviet-Nazi Pact that allowed Hitler to dismember Poland. Then they shifted the partly line to preach isolation and peace. Then they switched back to anti-Nazi talk and an insistence on an immediate Second Front when Hitler attacked his erstwhile ally. They also managed to ignore the frequent reports, all true, of the slaughter of the Russian intelligentsia, middle class, and Jews by the Stalinist police.

During the war, I was what I would call a conscientious murderer. I think I was a decent person, but history placed me in the position of having to kill other men. I hated it, but I did it with as much efficiency as I could. Under similar circumstances, I would do it again. There was no other answer to the Hitler nightmare but war. Otherwise, not even a small remnant of Jews would have been rescued. The American Jews would have followed the same path within a decade. No war can be a "good" war, but this was as close to one as a war can come. Our leaders, driven by their own greed, ambitions and fears, led us down the path to war. It took the blood, toil and sacrifice of the common people to bring some measure of sanity and progress back to the world—as it always does.

The Brief Tale of Greta

The reason for this story is a photo, long-lost but never quite forgotten, which turned up in my files as I was culling things to throw away. It is a hand-colored black-and-white photo of a lovely young woman who was my girlfriend for three years, from about 1937 to 1939. We saw each other frequently and we made plans about the future, in great detail. Since I worked six days a week at my father's store and my own and also went to college at night, we could only see each other on Sundays. I can't recall a Sunday when we did not meet, with the possible exception of major Jewish holidays, when my presence was mandatory at the synagogue.

For the time, she was a tall girl, about five feet nine inches, with a spectacular figure and a radiant smile. Just looking at her photo now brings back some of the joy I felt when she was present and she smiled. I am still astonished that she cared for me. I do not remember any serious arguments or quarrels; I only recall her smiling. She was easy-going and liked my company, as I did hers, and she was impressed by my intellectual pretension.

We were both fairly poor, but I always treated, even though she had a job. She was not demanding. She was quite content to walk in the park, have a soda or attend the local movie. Going to the Howard Johnson's for a sundae was about the height of my expenditures. I remember a foolish comment I put in my diary. (I used to keep a diary until I found out that my mother was reading it.) I had written on one day that I had spent the sum of six dollars, but I also indicated that it was worth it. Consider that sum, when the subway cost five cents and my wages were 18 dollars for a 60-hour week.

She loved to walk in the nearby Bronx Zoo or the Botanical Gardens and recite dialogue from Ibsen plays. She desperately wanted to be an actress on the dramatic stage, but neither of us knew how one launched such a career. I recall one day, just after a heavy rainfall, when we walked into the lilac section of the Botanical Gardens. The fragrance of the blossoms was overpowering. The heavy wet branches and leaves bent over us like a bower and seemed to drip perfume on us. We walked alone, clutching each other tightly as we strolled. We got soaking wet, but neither of us noticed. I can't ever smell the scent of lilacs without reliving that day and that walk and the way I felt about Greta.

What happened? She wanted to get married and brought up the subject often. I agreed that it would be wonderful, but I knew if I married her and she became pregnant, that would end my hopes for completing college, even at night.

Even more important, she was not Jewish. While her father was a Jew, a hard-drinking union organizer and socialist, her mother was a German Protestant, though not much of a churchgoer. The mother liked me, but the father was completely indifferent to me, except once when he warned me that a Jew marrying a *shiksa*, a non-Jewish woman, would have many problems.

While my father knew I was seeing her, since she lived only a few blocks away on Southern Boulevard, I knew that he would adamantly refuse to entertain the absurd idea that she could ever be a suitable daughter-in-law, even if she converted. All socialists were communists to him and I could not see how I could ever persuade him to accept that family as *machtunim* [in-laws]. Deep down I may have feared that the low aspirational level of her family would hold me back.

So, using the typical coward's way out, I procrastinated. I would soothe Greta and make half-promises and half-denials. She became angry and would demand more substantial evidence of my intentions. After all, she was over 20 and most of her girl friends were married. Being an "old maid" was a serious problem and a fate women strenuously tried to avoid, even if it meant marrying someone not quite suitable.

One day I received a note from her telling me not to call on her again. She was now going steady with another local young man, a Jew whom I knew and thought not much of a catch. Since I was not serious, she was doing the proper thing for her future.

I rushed over to her home, but she refused to see me and I went home quite despondent. As I think back, I realize that I never even discussed the situation with my parents, because I felt they would be grateful we were no longer together rather than sympathetic.

She married the other guy and I even sent her a small wedding gift, which I learned later she concealed from her spouse. I was terribly wounded, but the pain receded as I dated other women. I moved along with my life.

The war started. I went to work at General Motors at a startlingly (to me) high salary that was the envy of my friends, and the experience opened my eyes to a vast new world outside of the Bronx.

I lost track of her.

About two years later, I met her again and we walked and talked as we had in the past. She told me that her husband had been drafted. She did not like him at all and she was very unhappy. She asked if we could resume our friendship with the intention of getting married as soon as she could arrange a divorce.

I was shocked, because I had old-fashioned and romantic ideas about love and marriage. Her husband was away fighting and risking his life, and I was supposed to steal his wife so that she could write him a deadly "Dear John" letter. My dismay must have shown and she dropped the matter. She gave me her address and phone number. Somehow I lost the paper the first day, and I never saw or heard from her again.

Over the years I forgot her last name and her address. But I knew the building where her parents had lived. One day, when I was working in the Bronx, I went out of my way to see the places I had known and lived in three decades earlier. Most of the buildings were gone and so was her apartment building. It was a strange feeling. The lots were deserts of concrete rubble, and there was no sign of the noisy, lively throngs that used to walk those streets and inhabit those apartments. The place was gone and she was gone—forever. I never even considered trying to trace her.

But there are times when I wonder, idly curious, where she is, if she is alive, how her life turned out, if she had children, and how things might have been if I had married her.

It would have been a radically different life for me. I would not have completed school and would not have worked at General Motors. Without a college degree, my educational career would have been impossible, so I would have been a meat dealer or some other small entrepreneur or even a worker.

I do not believe that, much as I loved her, I would have been happy with such prospects. I always had higher hopes and dreams for myself. I was the only one of the 14 boys who hung out on the corner of Longfellow Avenue who completed college, and only two even started college, even with the GI Bill. I fear that our love would have cooled, and... who knows what would have happened.

Is this trite? Are there really eight million stories in New York City—worth reading?

The Fiddle

They both lived in the Bronx and they both hated it.

She, pressed by her intense fox terrier of a mother, sought to get away from the Bronx using her talent with the violin. He dreamed of being a grand entrepreneur who would buy his way out of the crowded vulgarity of the East Bronx with his business acumen.

They made a most unusual couple. He was strong and stocky, and he thrust his way through the world like a bulky ship cleaving the waves. She was slender and tall, taller than he, and willowy, with a sweet graceful manner and rather plain features. He talked loudly and confidently to conceal his feelings of inadequacy, his fear of not belong to her world, while she spoke shyly and softly, as if in fear of giving offence.

Their worlds were different. She went to Julliard and spoke of a brilliant, cultured world inhabited by Sol Hurok and Gregor Piatigorsky, while he went to evening college. During the day he lived in a world of burly, foul-mouthed men who slaughtered cattle and dismembered beef.

Yet both lived on the same block in the Bronx. For her, given her mother's frantic ambitions, the neighborhood was a trap, the result of her father's inadequate income. For him, the block was a proud step up in his immigrant family's saga. His father was proud of their address. Her mother shrank with shame when she was forced to mention it.

He liked her, while he still liked other girls. One of his other girlfriends later became a Metropolitan diva. But she impressed him the most, especially when she would pick up her violin and tuck it under her sweet, but weak, chin, and change. In a moment she turned from a shy, quiet girl into a magnificent musical instrument. With her violin cradled between hand and chin, her shoulders, fingers, wrists and elbows would move in a swaying ballet with the bow from which flowed the most inexpressibly beautiful music. She was no longer the unobtrusive person he knew, she was a scintillating, unobtainable fount of beauty.

From the time he attended her sweet-sixteen birthday party, carefully and frugally bringing her a box of Loft's candy, at which her mother cruelly sneered, it was known that they were going together. Despite her mother's constant efforts to break up the couple—she always called him the butcher—the girl persisted in going steady with him. Unwilling or unable to face her mother down, she would weakly defend her choice by frequently mentioning that he went to college at night. This was an obvious step above his friends, who spent their free time at the burlesque houses or the pool halls. Her mother was not impressed. Covered over with counterfeit, polite phrases, it was open war between her mother and him, with the girl as the prize, the fortress to be conquered.

She knew he was different from the quiet well-spoken boys she met at Julliard and that he really wasn't suitable, but she grew faint when he laughed and came close to her and she quivered when he touched her. He played the strong man, but he was quite impressed with her, even afraid of her, because her high opinion of him was crucial to his inner image.

Despite his loud hilarity, he realized that she was privy to a colorful, sophisticated world that was completely alien to the

East Bronx, much less the narrow streets of Bukovina, from which his family had immigrated. She was going to be both his prize possession, to prove his worth, and his passport into that glittering world.

He knew that his street corner gang, even though most of them were Jewish boys she knew from her high school days, would repel her. And why not? Their idea of humor was to see who could belch or break wind the loudest and their idea of a really clever joke was to crouch down behind someone so that another ruffian could push him over, to howls of laughter.

So to maintain some sort of contact, he would escort her to her world. There she was admired as an outstanding violinist, on a scholarship, and regarded as having enormous potential, a future female Heifetz.

There he was mute.

Her friends, some suitors, circled her like moths, speaking charmingly and knowledgeably, in cultured tones, of Mozart and Haydn or of their friendships with Arturo or Gregor or Lenny. Each charming and probably fictitious anecdote was greeted with restrained but lilting laughter and comments like "Doesn't he just?" or "Wouldn't you know?" or "Don't you just adore him?"

They were careful to observe whether he was impressed. He refused to be intimidated or show his awe openly, but he was impressed and it was reflected in his hangdog demeaner.

It was obvious from their covert glances and their giggling comments to her, that they were making sport of him. Aware of the way his muscles swelled his jacket, they were also very circumspect and took care not to make their comments too audible or too pointed. She strove valiantly to defend him and give him status. She would ask one or two of the other suitors to move aside, so that he could join the center of the magic ring that encircled her. She would lean toward him, smiling, so that all could see that she thought well of him. He was grateful for her concern and angry that he needed her protection.

Whenever the topic turned to music, he was totally out of his depth. He knew nothing about Beethoven or the quality of a Guarneri violin. But he ground his teeth and resolved to learn something about these esoteric aspects of life on this alien planet. Her friends, however, did not play fair. Just as soon as he learned to say something relatively correct about a classical composer, they switch the discussion to other even more esoteric areas, like the contrapuntal qualities of Copeland or the dissonances of a twelve-tone composition, and they would smirk at his bewilderment.

It soon became obvious that neither was happy in the other's world, so they carved out their romance in neutral places. They held hands in Howard Johnson's as they sampled each of the 37 flavors. They walked along the Grand Concourse or strolled the Botanical Gardens, where one wet and windy day they walked through an arbor of wildly thrashing lilac bushes. The scent of the blossoms and the presence of his beloved moved him greatly. He pulled her close and kissed her. She, still shy, responded with warmth. Their understanding deepened. The thought of going further never occurred to him. Not with a Jewish girl! Certainly not with a Jewish girl with such ambitions.

He loved to go horseback riding and went almost weekly, probably because the jodhpurs and boots he strode about in were so foreign in comparison to the usual Bronx costume. He offered to teach her how to ride. Her mother, knowing the girl had an important concert scheduled, adamantly refused to let her go. One Sunday morning, she sneaked out of her family's apartment and he met her with appropriate riding clothes he had borrowed from a friend. They hastened to the riding academy.

He selected a staid and quiet mare and carefully instructed her in the proper way to mount, how to hold the reins and how to direct the animal. He protectively rode close to her, stirrup to stirrup, as she cautiously left the stables and fearfully rode the horse out onto the bridle path, which adjoined a public highway.

She was pale, tense and easily startled, but grew in confidence as the animal and she seemed to develop some sort of rapport. She relaxed enough to consider a slow trot. The horse responded with a slow rolling canter that was easy, even for a beginner.

Just then an automobile passing close on the highway emitted a stentorian blast from its horn, and her startled horse lurched forward and started to race down the path. Frantic to halt the animal, she pulled back violently on the reins, and the horse halted sharply. She flew over its head and landed on the dirt path.

He was racing after her and her horse, when he saw her fall directly into the path of his running animal. A strong and skilled rider, he yanked back on the reins. His horse reared up and its hooves came down on the side of the path, away from her. She was looking up and saw this apparition, this golden knight on a rearing horse, surrounded by an aura from the sun behind him, coming to her rescue. Her heart melted completely in gratitude and admiration.

He brought his horse to a halt, slid from the saddle, and rushed over to her, earnestly looking at her face for signs of injury.

"I'm all right, I think," she said to assure him. "I fell on my hands and only my wrists hurt.'

"Her wrists," he thought. "With a concert in a few weeks, her mother will kill me."

He helped her to the side of the path, mounted his horse and retrieved her animal, which was now quietly walking back to the stables. He helped her up and she checked herself out for injuries. She has a bruise here and there and her wrists still hurt, but she seemed fine. She refused to remount her horse, no matter how often he repeated the old saw, "You have to get back on immediately or else you will never ride again." She still refused, so he dismounted and the two walked back to the stables. She leaned on him. While he liked the pressure of her body, he noted that she was limping a bit.

"Are you hurt?" he asked.

"No, I don't think so."

"What will we tell your mother?" he asked.

"We won't tell her a thing."

"Lots of luck. Just try to outwit that gimlet-eyed ferret," he thought. "She'll spot the problem in an instant."

And so it was. No sooner did he bring her back to her apartment, then the door swung open and her mother shrieked, "*Vey iz mir.* [Woe is me.] What happened to you? You are hurt!" Her hateful, basilisk glance demolished him, and he left the girl in her mother's loudly complaining care.

The next days were ones of intense anxiety. The doctors and the X-rays had indicated that there were no fractures and that her wrists had only suffered severe sprains. While all were relieved, that still left the question of the concert, especially since she would be unable to practice much prior to the event.

Her mother was venomous in her anger, even visiting his parents to denounce their son for leading her daughter astray and ruining her future prospects.

His parents, unable to follow her rapid flow of English, were certain that the girl was pregnant.

"Dun't vurry. It's not zo *geferlich* [terrible]," said the father. "He is a decent boy. He will marry her!" He was startled and confused when this reasonable assurance only brought forth even more volcanic anger. As the mother hastily departed, she swore never to let her daughter go out with that careless *trombenik* [bum], that *balaugoula* [common laborer], that *grubyan* [coarse person] It was interesting to hear that despite her dainty airs, the mother still resorted to Yiddish phrases and curses when under stress.

However, youth and good care brought the girl's wrist swellings down quickly and she recovered the flexibility she needed to perform. Her concert was a brilliant success. He felt even more outclassed than before.

Her mother would still not forgive him. Her father was grateful to the boy because his wife's termagant tantrums were directed toward someone else for a change.

So the girl, still enraptured by her vision of the rescuing golden knight, arranged her days and her rehearsals so that each Sunday she was able to slip away and walk and talk with her love.

They began to plan for the future. Depression-era children, their goals and plans were limited. He dreamed of a job that paid $100 dollars a week, steady. She, with a wider horizon, planned to have him serve as her manager, while she toured the capitals of Europe and earned enough for them to have a suite at the Plaza and first-class passage on the Queen Mary.

When the matter of a formal engagement was raised, he offered to buy her a diamond ring, as big, or bigger, than he could afford. When she questioned him about the amount of money involved, he reviewed his financial status and said $1,000, to him a stupendous sum. When he saw her face fall, he hastily said, "Well, $1,500."

Her face broke into a broad smile. "Great! One of my teachers at Julliard has a connection and he can get me a good—not top of the line—but a good Amati violin for that money. I would rather have that as an engagement present than a ring. What do you say?"

What could he say? He was surprised because the request was so unusual. He was supposed to be in love and this was what his love desired. So he agreed.

His mother was outraged. "*Vus far a gelobter geshenk iz dus?*" [What kind of betrothal gift is that?] A ring was traditional. It betokened a definite marriage and it also served as last-ditch savings, capital in time of financial distress. Who knew from fiddles?

While they were planning the event and enjoying the World's Fair, the winds of war blew in and everyone's attention was directed toward worrying about relatives caught behind the embattled armies.

But a promise was a promise. Gathering his resources, borrowing heavily from his parents, he went with her as they purchased the object of her desire: an Amati. He now knew enough about violins to know that not only was this a rare and beautiful instrument, but also that they were getting a real *metziah* [bargain].

It was time for an engagement party. After all, the gift had been given and it was the duty of her parents to recognize that a *shidduch* [match] had been arranged.

He wanted a few of his friends to attend, so he asked Heshie and Lippy and several others to come to the party. It was a mistake.

At the party, his street-corner gang, irritated by the snobbish disapproval of her friends, carried on even more outrageously than usual. They spilled the punch, devoured the food, and laughed raucously at inane jokes and double-entendres. Then Heshie discovered the violin case.

He removed the precious instrument and said, "What's so great about this? It looks like any other fiddle." And he tossed it to Lippy.

The knight, yelling in anger, ordered Lippy to "hand it over—immediately!"

Lippy tossed the violin to another member of the gang.

Pandemonium broke loose. The girl cried, the mother shrieked, the gang howled with cruel laughter, and the violin flew about the room like a demented bird.

Until one of the gang stumbled and fell heavily on the violin.

The noise of the violin smashing cut through all other sounds like a knife. The room grew totally quiet as one of the gang held up the broken violin, with parts dangling like an eviscerated chicken. The girl shrieked again and swooned.

He charged at Heshie and hit him in the mouth, shouting, "You bastard!"

"Hell," yelled Heshie. "Can't you take a joke? That's not her fiddle. I bought one for ten bucks at the pawn shop and switched it."

Everyone was stunned as another of the gang drew forth the real, and untouched, Amati. Smiles began to emerge and giggle of relief were heard. The girl, now recovered, snatched her precious violin back like a mother salvaging a child from the claws of a tiger. Clutching it to her breast, cradling it from the careless beasts that wanted to harm it, she crooned at it as she examined it.

Then she shrieked, "This is not my violin. You broke the real one by mistake!"

"You smashed my Amati, you vandals, you criminals. I'm going to have you all arrested!"

The entire party was shocked into silence again. An almost palpable feeling of horror enveloped the crowd. The gang, stricken with guilt and panic, could not stand to look at her blazing face and fled from the scene, leaving the sobbing girl and her irate parents.

Pale with anger, anxiety and contrition, he approached her and murmured, "Gee, I'm sorry, honey. Don't your folks have insurance? We can get another one."

She slowly looked up, gazed at him for a long moment, and then broke into a happy smile.

"They really broke the cheap one. This is my violin, my Amati. I just wanted to give them the same scare that they gave me. Don't tell them for a few days. Let them suffer for a while."

The party, exhausted by the rapidly changing events, soon disbanded. The story of the wrecked violin was the subject of much neighborhood levity for weeks. But her mother used it as her constant theme to break up what she considered an unsuitable match. "How can you associate with a man who comes from that element?"

She would not break off the engagement, but she agreed to delay the wedding, especially since she was now on tour and needed to be free for all possible concert dates.

He was upset about the delay because it indicated a reluctance on the girl's part. But he could not blame her after the shenanigans of the engagement party. So their plans were put off for a year. *Der mensch tracht und Gott lacht.* [Man plans and God laughs.]

Suddenly they did not have a year.

Their plans were altered by the army draft. He was unfortunate enough to have a low number and was one of the first to be called. He pressed her to get married before he went off for training, but her mother objected.

"What kind of marriage is that? Chasing him from one army camp to another. Going with him would ruin your promising career. What if he went overseas? What if he didn't come back? You would be a widow and at your age."

So the wedding was put off until he returned, but she promised to be faithful and wait for him. Immediately after his basic training, he returned and demanded that she marry him before he went overseas. She looked at him sorrowfully and said she could not, not yet at least. She was going to Boston for a concert and could not have a suitable wedding just then.

As he escorted her and her mother to the railway station, the girl sighed and cried and begged him to forgive her for the delay. Her mother sat quietly, but her eyes gleamed with satisfaction. As they arrived at the station and waited for her train to depart, the girl handed him her violin case and with a tremulous voice said, "Here, I return it to you."

Her mother objected, but she silenced her with a ferocious glance, and screamed, "This is what you always wanted!"

"Take it back!" she cried, and fled aboard the train. Her mother followed her and looked back triumphantly.

Stunned, he realized that more than a delay was involved. This was the breaking of a commitment. She was returning her precious Amati rather than go through with the marriage.

As the train pulled out, he sighed deeply with unhappiness, and then even more deeply with relief.

He knew the two would never be truly happy. He really had

wanted to break it off many times, especially since he had met someone more to his taste and values, but he was afraid she would not give him his fiddle back.

She went on to years of declining minor triumphs and eventually discarded the concert circuit to have a childless marriage with a dentist in Boston.

He used the money he got for the fiddle as an initial investment from which he developed a large business enterprise. He married a sturdy down-to-earth woman and had four children. They moved to Kings Point, where they laughed with gusto, fought noisily, and loved each other deeply for fifty years.

The Girl with the Gloves

It was a hot summer morning as he stood on the almost empty train platform. It had been a long and exhausting night shift at the General Motors plant in Tarrytown and he was bone tired. He was unfamiliar with the train and its schedule, because he always traveled to and from work in his elderly Pontiac. This day it was in the shop, undergoing rejuvenation, so he was forced to rely on alternative transportation to get back home, from Westchester to the Bronx.

Tired and dirty, annoyed by the brilliant sunshine, he slouched against the rear wall of the station and looked the length of the dusty, splintered, wooden platform.

That was when he noticed her. She was about 18 years old and stunningly turned out all in white or light-colored clothing. She wore a large white summer straw hat that sheltered her white skin from the sun. Her dress was some light, flowing fabric that seemed to surround her rather than cover her. Her shoes were shapely but sensible white oxfords. Yet he realized that despite the apparent simplicity, this was an expensive outfit.

Her lanky blond *shiksa* [non-Jewish woman] hair escaped from under her hat and lay on her shoulders. On her hands she wore gleaming white doeskin gloves. She wore no jewelry, except for a small delicate gold watch, and no makeup that he could discern. She had a thin book of poems under one arm and a small white purse swung from her other arm. She was a vision totally unfamiliar to a Jewish boy from the Bronx.

Like most upper class shiksas, she seemed unaffected by the heat and did not sweat at all. He, on the other hand, felt singularly scruffy. His clothes were dirty and his shirt stuck to his back. He needed a shave and his hands bore the grease and dirt that accompany work on the assembly line.

He was fascinated by the immaculate white gloves, even though most women in the 1930s wore them whenever going someplace. She even wore white stockings with her white shoes. No lady went out bare-headed, bare-handed or bare-legged in those days. Hats, gloves and stockings were essential in order to be appropriately dressed.

He lacked the chutzpah to approach her, so he watched her covertly as they both waited for the arrival of the train. He was careful not to approach her for fear of frightening her or for the greater fear that she would say something insulting. He didn't have the courage to sidle up to her, much less say anything to her. He knew his Bronx accent would grate harshly on her ears. In his mind, she was too far above him for him to even dream of a relationship.

At first, she did not look at him. When she did, she looked right through him. He realized that to her, he was invisible, too insignificant to snub. So he gazed at her raptly, almost worshipfully, from a distance. She was the ideal that appeared in all of the magazines of the times. She was what every young American male and most Jewish young males of the time dreamed of. She was straight out of *Esquire* or a Norman Rockwell painting or the Andy Hardy series. While she was his ideal, he knew that he was far from hers!

She took one glove off in order to get something out of her

purse. Just then a train heading north pulled into the station. He knew that it wasn't his, because the Bronx was south of Tarrytown. But she obviously was waiting for it and began to adjust her purse and book in order to step up into the train. She would be going up to one of the upper-class schools along that railway line, Vassar or Smith or perhaps an Ivy League school in Connecticut or Massachusetts.

Her train pulled in and she stepped aboard. In those days the train doors had windows for the upper half and they were usually left open, especially in the summer. As she stepped up, she was unaware that she had dropped the glove she was carrying. He noticed it and rushed forward to retrieve it for her. By this time the door had closed, though the upper window was still open.

Then, in a noble gesture, she snatched the other glove from her hand and tossed it out onto the splintered platform, where it rested next to its mate. What she seemed to be saying was that if she could not wear them, at least let someone else find a pair.

The young man, enchanted by the girl and her gesture, dashed forward, picked up both gloves and tried to throw them both back into the moving train. The gloves missed the open window, struck the side of the train and fell onto the dirty track. Blue-eyed, she looked at him with amusement, or contempt, and then disappeared from his sight on the rapidly moving train.

He climbed down from the platform to retrieve the soiled gloves from the track. As he climbed back onto the platform, he looked longingly down the track where her train had disappeared. Every aspect of the incident was indelibly burned into his mind and his memory.

Even though he had rarely used the train before, he now

made it his business to travel to and from work on it. He tried different times and different days, hoping to meet her again. He even resisted a shift switch so as to continue to use the train in the mornings. But he did not see her.

He wondered if she was a visitor who rarely used that train. Perhaps she had moved away or had altered the time she used the train.

Time after time he sought her. He even asked the stationmaster about the girl. The stationmaster laughed at him. "We get lots of them. They're on the way to and from the colleges or sorority weekends. I haven't any idea who she could have been."

Throughout the disappointing months he carried her gloves, now properly cleaned and carefully wrapped in tissue paper inside a box, in the hopes of returning them to her. Surely she would be impressed by such a gallant gesture! But he never saw her again.

Once his sister found the gloves in his dresser and asked if she could wear them on an important date. He was furious and adamantly refused. So the gloves lay, quietly yellowing in his drawer through the years.

Now that more than a half century had passed, he realized that it was a rare week that went by without remembering the image of that erect white-clad figure standing on that sunny platform. He often wondered what had happened to her. Was she happy? How had her life turned out? Was she still alive? Did she, this shiksa, know that a nice Jewish boy, who had never heard her voice, thought of her often? That he was still single and would love her till he died?

The Interview

"I don't think I have a chance, Mr. Dougherty."

"Of course you do," said the plant superintendent. "You have a terrific record here. In the short time since you joined General Motors, you've moved up quickly. Besides, what can you lose?"

"I could look like a fool if they turn down my application. I have enough enemies around here, without giving them something new to cause hostility toward me."

"Look, Max," said Mr. Dougherty. "You trust me, don't you?"

"Completely, Mr. Dougherty. You've been good to me and very helpful in my career here at GM."

He thought back to the time when, as a mechanic's helper on the assembly line, he had spotted Ralph Dougherty as a comer in the supervisory ranks and had hitched his wagon to Dougherty's star. It had been a brilliant move. Dougherty had accepted him and had found him to be an efficient assistant. He became Max's mentor. As Dougherty moved up the ranks, from foreman to general foreman and on to plant superintendent, he had pulled Max up behind him. Max took over each vacated position as Dougherty moved up ahead of him, traveling on Dougherty's coattails.

"Look, Max, I trust you, as you trust me. I know that you think I pulled you up the ladder. But you helped me climb. You made me look good. I could always depend on your department or your shift for pulling me out of a hole. You know how to organize people and production layouts and get the best out of them. You have a college background, even if it was only night school, and you know the union contract and the grievance procedures better than anyone in the shop. You can do the job."

"Thanks, Mr. Dougherty, but you know the real reason I can't get the job. Not everyone's like you."

"Why not? Just because you're Jewish? The world is changing. Old ideas are dying out. Efficiency, profits, costs—the bottom line is what counts today. You need a college education and you need to know something about engineering, union contracts and accounting. Old assembly-line dogs like me are going out of style. It's young, bright guys like you who will go far in the future. If you can produce, you can be a Hindu as far as the bosses are concerned. I never thought I could reach this position. Who would have thought it? I'm more than satisfied when I think of so many of my old buddies still busting their backs working the line."

"Well, Mr. Dougherty," Max said with a grin, "now I know why you are sending me to Flint. So I won't push you out of your job before you're ready to go."

"You bastard," said Mr. Dougherty, with a smile. "Don't think the idea hasn't occurred to me. I remember the first day you came to my attention. You, a mere leadman, were chewing out your own foreman for being incompetent. I gave you his job because you were right and I needed an S.O.B on the line. But I never forgot what I said to you at the time: 'I'd sure hate to be on your hit list!'"

"Thanks for the compliment, but I don't think you ever regretted being my boss. I never did anything that would hurt you or make you look bad."

"You're right, but now I know I won't go any higher and you still can be a real bigwig at GM. So take a chance. I'll write a strong letter of recommendation to go with your application."

Max prepared his application in response to the letter that had come to all supervisors from GM's central headquarters in Flint, Michigan. The Chevrolet division, undergoing some radical personnel changes, was in need of a strong executive to take over the newly created position of executive assistant to the president of the division, with the pay and benefits of a vice president. It was a plum position that, in one bound, bypassed all of the intermediate steps in the rigid GM hierarchy. It was like a parish priest being directly elected to the College of Cardinals. Max knew that hundreds of supervisors, afflicted with delusions of adequacy, would apply for the job.

But what the hell, what did he have to lose? Besides, Dougherty promised to keep the matter a secret, so that if he were rejected, as he was sure to be, no one would be the wiser.

He dispatched his application, buttressing it with several pertinent comments about his varied and successful experience in the company. After all, he had worked on all parts of the assembly line, from chassis to upholstery, had studied blueprinting, and had taken over the bomber-wing assembly department when they switched over to defense contracts. He hoped that his broad knowledge would overcome the basic handicap of being only 23 years old, which constituted extreme youth in the eyes of the hidebound leaders of the company.

And then he waited.

Several months went by and Max assumed that the matter was dead, although no announcement about an appointment had been made. One afternoon, he was called to Mr. Dougherty's office, where Ralph delightedly handed him a slip of paper.

"Please report to headquarters in Flint, Michigan, for a screening interview."

After that, the details about transportation, housing and expenses were a blur.

"In two weeks," he shouted with glee. "I'll have to get ready."

"How are you going to get ready?" asked Mr. Dougherty. "You don't know what they'll ask you."

"Well," said Max, "I'll brush up on the union contract and I'll check over some of my suggestions about how to improve the Chevrolet image and how to reduce costs. I've already started to grow a mustache, so I'll look older."

"God, you are some piece of work," said Ralph. "Good luck! And don't forget who put you there, when you are eating in the executive dining room in Detroit."

And the day came to pass. Max was directed to a private airfield in Westchester where a company plane took him on his first plane ride to the airport outside of Flint. There he was taken by company car to a nice hotel, where he spent a sleepless night filled with anxiety and apprehension.

The following day he was driven to GM headquarters in Flint. The building was overwhelmingly imposing. He had seen pictures of it often in the company literature, but had never thought that he would ever visit it.

He was courteously ushered into a large waiting room where about twenty soberly dressed men were waiting. As he arrived, they all looked up and appraised him carefully. He realized that they were his competition, and every one was close to, or over, 40 years old. He had no chance against a battery of men as experienced as these guys.

The men were called in turn to another room, where they stayed from ten to 30 minutes. Each returned pale and in varying degrees of composure. Each refused any comment about the ordeal. Finally came the turn of Max, who was feverish with anxiety.

As he entered the room, he was startled by the sight of several very high-ranking GM officials seated at a large mahogany table, presidents of the various divisions, as well as the president of GM himself, Harlow Curtis. It was as though a new lawyer were introduced to the whole black-clad Supreme Court at one time. These were not people, these were demigods! He was struck mute.

"Sit down, young man," said one of the gods, kindly. "What is your name'?"

There was a long and uncomfortable pause.

"I forget," said Max miserably, "but it will come to me. It will come to me!"

The rulers of the wheels of America smiled at each other, but were courteous enough to continue the interview. Max, realizing that the interview was now a total loss, relaxed completely. What worse could happen to him'?

And so, fluently and casually, he discussed union grievances and offered some fresh insights into future union negotiations. He also offered ideas on alterations in the way an assembly line should be manned. The interview period lengthened and the group seemed quite interested, even asking where he had gained his expertise on the union contract.

"I used to be a shop steward," he told the startled group.

"How did you get from the union side to the management side?"

He started to respond by saying that he thought that the management side would offer better rewards, when he loudly blurted out, "I remember!"

"You remember what?"

"I remember my name! I told you it would come to me!"

The group dissolved into laughter and the interview was terminated. Max never remembered how he left the room or reached home the next day.

The other candidates were alarmed at the hilarity that came from the interview room, thinking it betokened the election of a new crown prince.

They were wrong. Though no reason was ever cited, Max was not selected.

But the bigwigs never forgot that candidate, and every time one visited the plant in Tarrytown, he never failed to ask to meet the young man who didn't remember his own name.

Ralph was more disappointed than Max, but both settled down to their routines quite calmly. One morning, Max entered the superintendent's office to find Ralph sorrowfully looking at a pink slip. He handed the slip to Max, who read that Ralph, after more than twenty years of devoted service, was being discharged. With benefits, of course, but discharged long before he was ready. The new superintendent was to be one of Max's rivals, another general foreman. Max realized that no matter how high he climbed in the company ranks, someday that would be him reading a pink slip. He'd be cast aside like a used-up dray horse. He realized that he could not devote his life to a company that preached loyalty, but did not practice it.

Max and Ralph left the plant about the same time, Ralph to retirement and Max to start his own business.

World War II

The Night the Japanese
Bombed the Bronx

In January 1942, immediately after Pearl Harbor, the American public was beside itself with self-generated fears, bordering on panic, that the Japanese would soon invade the mainland. The stunning capabilities of the Red Ball bombers of the Rising Sun gave credence to the idea that they could, and possibly would, bomb us at will.

My father, who had served in two wars, lived through a revolution, immigration to the U.S. and the Great Depression, always adopted the worst possible scenario for any event. He collected disasters like other people collected souvenirs. He always foresaw death, doom and destruction.

He was a professional worrier. Let a child be ten minutes late coming home and he would call the police and the local hospital. If you were 30 minutes late, he would call the morgue. No one dared to be more than an hour late, because that provoked a two-hour session of tirades and repetitions of "Where were you? Why didn't you call?" A rainstorm or a report of an accident in another city would bring stern reminders of "*gib achtung*" [take care]. He knew of every accident, no matter how weird or unlikely, that had been reported by the press and made certain that we also knew of them and the moral attached: gib achtung or else.

But back to the Japanese. Since we lived on the sixth floor at the top of an East Bronx apartment house, my father felt that we were singularly vulnerable. Despite the many square miles surrounding us with identical roofs with their identical elevator shafts and clothes dryers, he was quite certain that our roof would be specially singled out by Japan. My father became the early warning system for the family as he listened for the Emperor's bombers.

While the skies were less trafficked than they are today, commercial flights such as the Yankee and China clippers operating out of Flushing Bay, mail planes and some private and military aircraft did traverse the skies of the Bronx then.

About midnight we heard them. That is, Papa heard the enemy's bomber fleet making its first pass over the helpless city. Air raid sirens did not sound. That was not surprising, because they had not been installed yet. The nation was still shocked into immobility by the bombing of the Navy the previous month. Except for the hordes of young men signing up for the conflict, little had been done to protect the populace.

But my father was ready. "*Hehr, hehr* [listen, listen]," he said. "They are coming." A police siren wailing in the street below was woven into his impression and confirmed his diagnosis. The bombs would shatter our pleasant four-room abode and our home would take on the look of a gutted tenement in London, with the contents spilling obscenely into the burning streets. Not our family, if our fervid protector had anything to say about it. It was every family for itself.

"To the bunkers!" shouted my father.

"Papa, we have no bunkers."

"Then to the cellar!" shouted Papa. "Each take some money. If we are separated, we will meet at Uncle Abe's house."

I, over 20 and thinking myself an adult, demurred, but a ferocious glance from Papa quickly quelled my incipient rebellion. My sister, approaching womanhood, had greater success because she was pretty and his favorite.

"I won't go. I don't like it down there," she complained. She was a Jewish American Princess long before the term was coined.

The king considered the complaint of his princess. Any complaint that I would have made would have been discarded out of hand and I would have been given a *frask im punim* [smack in the face] for my temerity.

"Okay," he said. "Take along the best linens and blankets and we will be comfortable. No more. Let's go!"

My mother wasn't even consulted. We matched up blankets, bulky pillows and linens and fled into the hall. All five of us, clutching our bulky burdens, crowded into the small elevator and we descended into the basement. I was struck by the singular lack of panic among the 90-odd other families in the apartment building. All was quiet and serene in the clean hallways. No one was fighting us for space or priority in the elevator. If I did not know better, I would have thought that they were foolishly asleep and unaware of the terrible and imminent danger facing them. Death was sweeping down on them and they did not know it.

When we arrived at the basement, it was empty of people but full of vast boilers, huge sighing furnaces, clicking electric circuits, the gurgle of water through the mains and assorted dust and cobwebs. My father selected the least unattractive area and suggested we settle there.

"Not with my linens. Don't you dare put them down on that dirty floor," said Mama very firmly. While Papa was always the boss, he decided that this was not the time to challenge her. Her tone had a stridency that alerted him to the fact that she was close to the limit with his *narishkeit* [foolishness].

So we stood there, holding the linens off the floor. The Polish janitor, who guarded his boilers and dumbwaiters zealously, heard us talking and looked in on us. Seeing five woebegone figures holding white bundles, he silently withdrew. He knew that the Jews had some peculiar observance, but the was a new one to him.

So we stood there. An hour passed and not one bomb fell. We began to raise some objections. "I have to go to work soon!" "I have an exam tomorrow—I mean, today"

"Maybe they are bombing another section," said Papa. But it was obvious that the heart had gone out of him.

"Let's go up," he conceded.

Just for spite, the elevator stopped at every floor as we ascended. At each floor there were tenants, either late-shift workers or early risers, about to enter the elevator when they saw five pajama-clad people clutching pillows, and so they backed away. No one wanted to get involved with such obvious *meshugoim* [crazy people]. No one asked us anything and we were too haughty to deign to offer an explanation. I really don't know what we could have said. But little did they know that our alertness and prompt action had saved the population of the Bronx.

We arrived at our apartment and went to bed without any conversation. Later we would laugh hilariously about the night the Japanese bombed Longfellow Avenue, but that night we were too embarrassed and humiliated to see the humor in the situation. Papa never forgave the Japanese for their sneak attack… or lack of one.

Weekend Pass

Licari was always slow. Not really stupid, but no great brain, either. So when he called out, "Here they come!" everyone knew it was too late to do anything about it. They had set up Licari as an outpost to sound an early warning, so that they could do the final touch-up and last moment chores to get the barracks into top shape before the inspection. So when they heard Licari, they all rushed about the room, but it was too late, of course.

There were the officers, ready to commence the weekly inspection, and there were the officer-candidates, still holding brooms and mops in their hands.

"Ten-hup!" hoarsely bellowed the first sergeant, announcing the presence of the colonel and his entourage. All of the candidates hastily stowed away the cleaning gear and snapped to attention.

Ross, who had just come into the barracks after checking out the latrine, hastily reviewed his bunk and area to reassure himself that he could pass the high standards required of the Saturday morning inspection. He just had to get a pass for this weekend! He realized that he was still holding a mop and, unable to think of anything else, he "presented arms" with the mop. As he stood there stiffly, holding his frail "weapon" in front of him, the officers suppressed smiles.

Except the colonel. He had no smiles for Ross. He zeroed in on him immediately and directed him to "Get in front of your footlocker, soldier."

As Ross obeyed the command, he looked down into his footlocker and realized that there was an orange on display there. He had taken one for breakfast and deciding to keep it for future consumption, had brought it back to the barracks. Unable to find a place for it—it certainly could not be placed on his bed or his open shelves—he had thoughtlessly put it in the footlocker. There it was, glowing golden, absolutely incongruous in the drab surroundings of an army barracks. He was certain that it would act as a magnet for the colonel's eyes.

The officers moved down the center aisle of the barracks, led by the major with the colonel following. The latter loved to mark down demerits and penalties for the officer-candidates. As the officers moved down the ranks of erect and immobile soldiers, Ross reviewed his history at the Armored Forces Officers Candidate School (OCS) during the last few weeks.

Initially he had been praised and given plum assignments, map-making rather than garbage collection, because he was bright and responsive. Unfortunately, he was also a clown and had little respect for authority, particularly what he considered stupid authority. He should never have poked fun at Colonel Pearsall, but he could not resist such a pompous target.

The colonel, an old retread pulled off the National Guard retired list, was eager to impress the young candidates with his military bearing and experience. Neither was particularly impressive, because he had a heavy paunch and he had never heard a weapon fired in anger. Except for some brief time in a World War I training camp, he had gained his exalted status as a light colonel and commanding officer of a training battalion because of pull, seniority and the needs of a rapidly expanding army. He had never seen combat, and only through the sheer weight of years had he been promoted to lieutenant colonel. It was a rank he neither deserved nor could effectively fill. Despite his high opinion of himself, the army was not stupid enough to give him command of troops in the field.

So the colonel, speaking in a heavy southern drawl, worked out his frustrations and military ferocity by lecturing his troops incessantly on the pettiest of topics. One of his pet tirades dealt with water discipline. Since the soldiers exercised in the enervating heat of Kentucky, the use, or misuse, of water was a serious matter. For some unknown reason, the colonel mispronounced the words as "waa-daa deseplin," as he constantly chided the soldiers for the overuse of water. He frequently supervised the amount of water used for drinking, showering and shaving, but did not go so far as to check the matter of toilet flushing or vehicle washing. He constantly stressed the need for water conservation. Although the rivers nearby were often overflowing, he ranted on about "waa-daa deseplin."

One afternoon in the barracks, Ross decided to imitate the colonel. Everyone was having a wild, hilarious time as Ross pranced through clever impressions of the colonel's mannerisms and shouted, "Di Zeppelin, di Zeppelin." Suddenly the barracks was deadly quiet. As Ross turned about, he saw the red-faced colonel glowering at him apoplectically. The narrow-minded, redneck colonel had never liked northerners and never like smart alecks, and to be made fun of by a smart aleck and a New Yorker, at that, really aroused his ire.

The colonel said nothing, but things got bad after that. Ross was placed on KP far more often that the usual rotation and was assigned night guard duty after a heavy day of training. Whenever there was a particularly dirty job, like cleaning a kitchen flue or moving trash or clearing a stuck drain, his name somehow appeared on the duty roster. It seemed that the first sergeant had a list of available soldiers for such jobs with only one name on it. His.

He was strong and he knew that training was only for a few more months and then he would be a "ninety-day wonder," an officer, even if only a lowly second looie, and away from Colonel Pearsall.

But worst of all, he was constantly getting demerits. The system was designed so that three demerits in one week meant no weekend pass. For the previous several weeks he had been denied a weekend pass, while his friends enjoyed the delights of Louisville, such as they were. He would stand, lonely and forlorn, feeling embittered and deprived, as all his buddies, clad in sparkling Class A uniforms, grinned on their way to the Louisville bus. "We'll tell you all about it, Ross," they shouted, as they happily departed for town. He was stuck on the post, and to make things worse, he would be assigned some onerous or demeaning task.

He tried to be a good soldier. He knew damn well that he was a better soldier and future officer than most of his buddies, but he was up against the system. The colonel had it in for him and the first sergeant and all of the other officers and non-coms took the hint and leaned on Ross. So he collected demerits like a vacuum cleaner collects dust. They found fault with him every day, in every way, to the point where there was a barrack's pool on how many demerits Ross would collect in one week. Thirty-seven was the winning number one week.

But not this week! This week was special. His wife had written that she had saved money and was taking the train down from New York to Louisville to spend the weekend with him. Since then, he had striven mightily to be the best damned soldier since MacArthur had graduated from the Point.

He never complained. He walked his post with dispatch and precision. He ate only square meals, in the mechanical manner that delighted martinets. His bed and footlocker were immaculate. His rifle sparkled and you could see your face in his gleaming shoes. He was courteous and obeyed every military regulation. His salute was snappy enough to please a Marine drill instructor.

Wonder of wonders, he did not receive one demerit the whole week. Even the noncoms prejudiced against him were impressed by his struggle to keep a clean record. For six entire days he had received not one demerit. His record was pristine. This week he would surely get his weekend pass. Even the colonel, cruel monster that he was, could not keep him from that prize, the cherished weekend pass.

As the colonel strode down the line, he looked carefully at the beds, the rifles, the way the footlockers were arranged and the manner in which clothing was displayed in closets. He gazed at the lavatories and the sinks and used his white gloves to check the immaculate windowsills. He marched up and down the line, examining each man and his gear in turn.

Finally he stood before the erect and perspiring Ross. "He'll see that lousy orange," thought Ross.

The colonel looked at Ross. He looked at the tautly made bed, the proper display of clean clothing and the sparkling high-shine shoes. A true spit-and-polish soldier! Pleased, the colonel started to turn away, when his eye was caught by the golden glint of the orange. The traitorous orange glowed luminously against the drab khaki underwear on display.

"What's this?" asked the colonel.

Major Tuchislecker stepped forward to enter the demerit in his log.

"Sorry, sir," said Ross, still holding his mop at present arms. "I improperly brought an orange back to the barracks after breakfast." He knew that an explanation or an excuse would not work. Perhaps a manly admission of error would.

"Humph," said the colonel and turned to the major. "One demerit for the unauthorized possession of groceries."

"Thank God," thought Ross. "One demerit still gets me the pass."

The colonel was not quite finished. "Another demerit," he said to the major, "for improper display of groceries."

"What the hell was the proper way to display unauthorized groceries?" thought Ross savagely. "But at least that's it. I still get the pass."

Ross began to sigh with relief. The colonel was about to turn away. He stopped, reached down, and touched the orange with his white glove.

With a smile, he said to the major, "Third demerit for dust on groceries." He looked at Ross with a wicked smirk, hoping that an explosion would grant him the chance to bust Ross out of OCS. Ross did not move a muscle or utter a sound, though his eyes blazed.

Disappointed, the colonel turned to the sergeant and said, "See that he is confined to post and be sure to collect his Class A uniforms. We can't have him slipping off the post."

And out they marched, the sergeant carrying Ross's uniforms.

Crestfallen, depressed and furious, Ross flung himself on his bed. The other soldiers laughingly left the barracks, clustered about the first sergeant, accepted their weekend passes and departed.

Ross sat on the bed and stewed and stewed. "Damn, I've got to get off this post. I've got to see my wife. She's coming all this way in wartime and I don't know how to contact her now. She won't know what happened to me. She'll be furious or frightened."

He knew he couldn't leave the post in his rumpled fatigues or work clothes. The first MP who saw him would arrest him out of hand. As Ross angrily wandered up and down the aisle, thinking, he recalled that Whitmore, who was about his size, had two Class A uniforms, as all of the soldiers did. Since Whitmore was out on pass himself, he wouldn't notice if Ross briefly borrowed his uniform.

Hastily, he donned the uniform. It fit fairly well, but if he stepped out of the barracks while the others who knew him were around, all hell would break loose. So he waited until he was sure that everyone had left the company area. If some of the company sergeants noticed him, they would instantly denounce him as a fraud. Once he had slipped over to a different company area, no one would know him in an encampment that had such a vast turnover of personnel every week.

The permanent cadre, those who were permanently stationed on the post, knew each other quite well. But the officer-candidates and the other armored force trainees came and went in 17-week cycles and did not know anyone outside of their own training battalion.

So he waited until it was dusk and then quietly strolled to the camp entrance. At the gate, the MPs were carefully checking each soldier for his pass, even the sergeants. He knew he had no pass and that if he was detected, he faced a hell of a problem. But still, the idea of his wife waiting warm and receptive for him in the city, while he sat amongst the pots and pans of the mess hall, filled him with rage and desire. He had to take the chance.

Just then, several officers' cars pulled up at the gate. The MPs were distracted and Ross slipped into a group that had been checked and were leaving the post.

Once he got off the post, Ross grabbed a taxi.

"Where to?" asked the driver.

Ross stammered, "To the railway station." And they briskly drove off to the depot.

Ross was familiar enough with the wiles and procedures of the army to know that if he put one foot into that station, the MPs would descend upon him with their unreasonable insistence on a valid pass. Rail stations and bus terminals were where the army could most easily locate and apprehend soldiers who were absent without leave.

So at first, he did not enter the station. But how to find his wife?

He kept peeking through the large glass doors of the station. Then he would dash into the station, check the arrivals board and hastily leave. The train bearing his wife was listed as three hours late, not unusual for wartime travel. Since he was also about three hours late, things were not too bad. He dashed in and out several times to check on the arrival time of his wife's train. His anxiety to avoid MP attention was making it impossible for the MPs not to notice him. However, he was now blinded by everything but his intense desire to see his wife.

Finally the board signaled the arrival of her train. He placed himself at an entrance nearest to the train arrival gate, so he could see his wife. And there she was! He had forgotten how beautiful, how desirable, she really was.

All restraint gone, he dashed up to her. She looked up, smiled, and without a word, they fell into a long, warm embrace.

He felt a tap on his shoulder. As he turned around, he thought, "My God! Where does the army get these hulking guys to serve as MPs?" There they were, two huge bookends, each the size of a refrigerator.

"Can I see your pass, soldier?" rumbled one of them.

"What? Sure. It's right here." He fumbled with his blouse pocket button. They waited patiently, having heard this ploy innumerable times.

"Oh, my God, I must have left it at the post!"

The other MP said, with bogus sympathy, "That means we will just have to take you back to the post, so you can get it, won't we?"

"What's going on?" inquired the young wife.

"Don't worry, ma'am," said one of the MPs, with elephantine chivalry. "This soldier is AWOL."

"What does that mean?" she asked.

"That means he is off the post without a pass, violating all of the regulations. He has to go back and he'll probably get some time in the stockade."

"May I talk with him for a minute?" begged the wife.

This was the south and politeness was a requirement, so one MP said, "Okay, but just one minute."

Ross said to her, "Please, stick around. I've reserved a room for you in the Brown Hotel. Please, stay there. I'll try to get out. Don't go back until I see you. I'll try to call you in any case. Maybe I can straighten this out when I get back to the post." And he gave her a quick kiss.

The MPs smiled and, taking a shoulder apiece, literally lifted Ross into the MP jeep. Off they went, leaving his disconsolate wife behind, abandoned, bag and baggage.

The MPs hauled him back to camp and delivered him to the

company headquarters. The toady company clerk immediately notified the colonel, who appeared promptly.

"Oh," he said, smiling with delight, "you didn't take my word for it. You defied my orders and went AWOL. Do you know what that means in time of war? That's desertion in the face of the enemy. You can be shot!"

Even the MPs realized that colonel didn't know what he was talking about. They were about three thousand miles from the nearest "face of the enemy," so the threat was absurd.

"All right," shouted the colonel. "I place you on company punishment. You are confined to barracks until tomorrow morning and then you will fall out and police up the entire company area. You are on permanent KP and you can forget about a pass until the end of your training. Out of my sight!"

Even more dejected and unhappy than ever, Ross went to his lonely, narrow cot with thoughts of his wife only 10 miles away, alone and crying, in a warm, fragrant hotel room.

The next morning he was rousted out of bed by one of the buck sergeants. "Up and at 'em, soldier. The colonel wants you policing up the place, bright and early."

There he was, raking up the leaves from the gravel walks and picking up cigarette butts and minor litter. He was making the area neat, orderly and sterile, just what the army loved. He was growing hot, weary and hungry. He had not had breakfast and he did not dare to ask whether he could stop work to eat.

Suddenly his name came over the regimental squawk box. "Ross, G. Company C, report to the adjutant's office! On the double!" The message echoed among the buildings.

He stopped to inquire from the company clerk what the message meant.

"Don't know a thing about it, Ross. Better get your butt over there."

"What now?" wondered Ross, as he raced to regimental headquarters. Probably they had decided that the colonel, who wanted to keep his battalion record clean, had not given him enough punishment. He had defied a direct order and had stolen a uniform. Probably he was facing a general court-martial. He would surely be bounced out of OCS now!

"Ross, G., reporting to the adjutant's office as ordered."

The adjutant, a major, returned Ross's salute and said, "Into the colonel's office. On the double!"

As Ross turned towards the commanding officer's office—this was a full bird colonel, not a light colonel like Pearsall—he thought, "This looks terrible. This really means heavy punishment. God knows what they will do to me now."

He approached the sergeant sitting outside the colonel's office. "Ross, G., reporting to the colonel's office as ordered."

"Go right in, Ross," said the sergeant somewhat diffidently. "Colonel Buford is expecting you."

Ross opened the door, walked in, saluted smartly, and said, "Ross, G., reporting, Colonel Buford, sir."

The colonel, a southerner who resembled Robert E. Lee and had carefully fostered that image, looked at him sternly and said, "Ross, I have special orders of the day for you. You will secure your Class A uniform and spend the day escorting this charmin' young lady about the post."

Ross was uncomprehending, stunned. As he glanced to his left, he realized that a women sitting in a comfortable chair was smiling at him. It was his wife!

"Yes, sir!" barked Ross, flinging the colonel a crisp salute. He raced back to his company headquarters, retrieved his Class A uniform from the sergeant and dressed hurriedly. He ran back to the regimental headquarters, embraced his wife and asked, "What happened?"

"When I heard from the chaplain that you had been put on company punishment, I didn't know what that meant. But when I learned that it meant you would be picking up cigarette butts, while I waited for you, I got very angry." She swelled up to her towering five-foot height.

"I got onto the post and went straight to the adjutant's office. I told them that I didn't come hundreds of miles, all the way to Kentucky, just to see my husband's backside as he bent over picking up butts. He thought it was hilarious and spoke to the colonel. I think I heard one of them refer to Pearsall as an asshole."

"Thank God, honey," he said. "You've saved my life. But I still don't have a pass."

"Yes, you do," said the tiny fighter. "The colonel gave me one for you. And to make up for my disappointment last night, you are to spend another night with me in Louisville and not report back until Monday."

"This is wonderful. Let's walk around the post first."

As they walked about, arm in arm, he showed her areas of interest, such as the parade ground and the rifle range, and then they came to the tank park.

"My God," she said. "How enormous they are."

"I can drive one of those. Would you like a ride?"

"Can you?" she asked fetchingly.

He knew he shouldn't, but in a state of wild euphoria, he said, "Of course! Let's go."

She clambered up into the monster machine with him. He checked the ignition and the fuel. He turned on the power and heard the gargantuan bellow, as the machine sprang into life. He put it into gear, slowly but correctly, and the tank moved forward. The tank moved right at his command, left at his command, and even stopped at his command. Although he had only a limited time in training on it, to his amazement, he knew how to drive it.

They went clanking heavily down the road, past his own company area. Looking out through the periscope he spotted the colonel's car, a red bucket of bolts. He stopped the tank as he considered the opportunity. Should he or shouldn't he run over it?

He started up the tank and approached the car, closer and closer. Then he changed his mind, deciding not to run it over, and turned away. But a tank is an unwieldy thing and it caught the side of the car as it turned aside. With the screech of tortured metal, the heavy tank tread scraped along the side of the car, removing both the front and rear left fenders, as well as the running board.

In the semi-deserted Sunday atmosphere of the area, no one appeared to have heard the accident. People were used to seeing and hearing tanks rumbling by. Ross continued on his way, eager to leave the scene of the disaster. Using another route, he returned the tank to the park, and they took off without being seen by any of the park personnel.

"Have I shown you enough of the post, Ma'am?" he saluted his wife.

"Sho' 'nuff, honeychile," she laughed. "Let's get to the hotel."

They spent a far different night than the one before.

Best of all, when Lt. Colonel Pearsall discovered that his car had undergone extensive renovation, he checked all of the tanks in the area, hoping to find one with the giveaway red paint. He found none. The colonel had his suspicions, but now that Ross seemed under the protection of the regimental CO, he carefully avoided any further entanglements with him.

The sergeant in charge of the motor pool had found one tank heavily decorated with the red clue. Fearing that he would be blamed for the unauthorized use of a precious vehicle, he had carefully removed all signs of the accident. The sergeant stoutly maintained that none of his tanks had left the park at any time that day. Since none were authorized to leave, therefore, by all army logic, none had left.

The Million-Dollar Wound

Being a veteran gives one the undeserved idea that, simply by surviving, one has something significant to recount. Surviving veterans meet and talk about war and combat, especially those purported to be the glorious parts.

I can't recall much glory, but I remember a lot of discomfort, boredom, anger, misery, bone-breaking fatigue and outright gut-wrenching fear. I think back on the days when my fear left me feeling so hopeless that I could barely function. I had a premonition, every day, that this would be the day I would buy the farm. Or worse, I would end up lying in a hold, shattered, mutilated and subject to the inept, insensitive ministrations of the medics. My own fears were so great that I had no pity for others.

Getting through another firefight without serious injury or death seemed a forlorn hope. During the fierce attacks that took place when we tried to rescue our besieged Company C and Company D from an enclave near Bastogne, the casualty rate of those killed, wounded or captured in two weeks was 40%, leaving the battalion with fewer than 700 men as "effectives."

So one could only hope that something would get you out of combat before the inevitable took place. Something: a million-dollar wound, a smooth capture by the enemy, or, best of all, reassignment away from the front. The first was difficult to arrange and self-wounding was treated with great severity by the authorities. The second was impossible for a Jewish boy. So all I could do was *daven* [pray] for the third, a shift away from the killed fields.

Every day our tanks rolled out of our overnight tank park, refueled and remunitioned, with their crews renewed with a fear-engendered reckless courage. We were so frightened that we often took rash risks just to get through this experience as soon as possible. We could see no way out. I contemplated racing my tank to the nearest Swiss border and hopefully sitting out the war as an internee. Wilmot, one of my tank-mates, was willing, but Porter, a Connecticut Yankee, refused. So we did nothing except turn our tank out every day, like bomber pilots going out on a feared mission.

I fell in love with my tank, a behemoth. Fully loaded with fuel, ammunition, spare parts, jerricans and tools, it was 44 tons of destruction on the loose. The Sherman tank had an ugly silhouette and menaced the enemy with the growl of its engine and the clanking of its heavy treads, as well as with its 76mm. cannon. I would hear its noise with affection because it was distinctive to me, and not one of "them," those others that threatened me with the rumble of war. It was a proud if heavy beauty that could safely remove me from harm's way.

Each identical machine became an individual to its crew, who knew its cranky ways and weaknesses. We soon festooned a new tank with gear: tents, recognition panels, loot, such as clocks and chairs. Ours bore an enormous cooking pot that looked like a witch's kettle and had served to boil laundry in some small French town. At each stop, we would light a cooking fire, set up the kettle and invite other soldiers to join us, provided they contributed something to our perpetual stew. Each would offer canned eggs, canned meat, a liberated chicken, some fresh vegetables snatched from a garden. All went into the pot. It tasted differently every day, but it always had one virtue—it was hot.

Some of the tanks, if the commanding officer was liberal, were decorated with paintings of semi-clad and very nubile women. My vehicle, for reasons I never learned, was called "Ash and Trash." Those who had painted the name on it were long gone when I arrived.

As soldiers, we matured in stages, in spasms, if you will. First the soldier tries to mask his fears and anxieties, because this is the way books and Tom Mix and Gary Cooper taught him is the only acceptable way for a "man" to act.

Second, he learns to detect and trust his unrooted and unspecified suspicions about incongruous silences, incongruent noises and intuitive alarms. He learns to jump before he hears the "incoming mail" of the enemy artillery shell. Finally he develops a perception, an almost radar-like skill of monitoring and interpreting data. His combat instincts, fertilized by fear, have become well honed.

All this has been learned over the bodies of his less fortunate buddies, and he hates the replacements who have taken their place. Each represents a buddy he trained with, drank with, boasted, laughed and loved with. Experienced soldiers at the front don't make friends easily with replacements. They learn to be friendly but uninvolved.

Most of the men who had originally come ashore with my battalion had long since departed: some via the drab coffins the grave registration men supplied, others to hospitals in England or home. Only the skillful, or the very lucky, or those who managed to stay far enough behind the lines had survived. The replacements arrived to become skillful, wounded or dead, as fortune decreed. The army starting calling them "reinforcements," because "replacements" had an unsettling connotation.

The repples (recent arrivals from the replacement depots were called repple dapples) thought that our coolness and reluctance to be friendly was a form of snobbery and reflected the elitism of the old timers. While they thought I was an arrogant pain in the neck, they clung to me because they thought I was their ticket home. Somehow, by surviving the destruction of several vehicles, in two cases caused by my own stupidity, I seemed clad in some sort of cloak of invulnerability that would shelter them, too.

I resented it when they clung to me, because I was worried about getting myself through. All I could think of was that death would come—soon. What an ambiguous word "soon" is. When is soon? One hour? One day? A year? Death comes haphazardly and plays with all soldiers without rhyme or reason, selecting one and ignoring another standing in the same place.

I recall a small, one-room schoolhouse on the German border. A pouring rain had just stopped when we pulled up directly in front of the school. We dismounted from our tanks and two of my friends ran in, went to the front of the room, and, delightedly, began writing on the chalkboard. I stood in the doorway and removed my wet poncho. Wilmot took one end of it and we started to fold it up when a mortar shell burst on the step outside. Instantly, the poncho turned into lace as the mortar fragments tore through it. Though there were even holes in the areas between our fingers, neither Wilmot nor I was scratched. When my head cleared from the explosion, I looked into the room. The other two soldiers, thirty feet away at the chalkboard, were both slumped on the floor. At first I could see no wound. Then I found that both their spines severed. Both were dead before they hit the floor. Death had played "eeny meeny miney mo" again.

After an incident like that, every survivor seeks some meaning in his survival, some hidden plan of God or destiny. While this experience can make a believer, or at least a pilgrim, of some, there is really no hidden meaning. Fate is fickle. It destroys some and leaves others unscathed. It is as meaningless as a series of random numbers used in statistics.

We never talked about our fear of death. Instead, we complained about minor things. I heard voluble and bitter bitching about the lack of fuel, long waits, poor food, wet ground, lack of mail, confusing orders, and on and on. I recall endless and meaningless conversations about the atypical. Everyone who was even slightly different—fat, thin, stupid, slow, Irish, Italian, Jewish, a hick—was kidded and teased mercilessly, perhaps to drown out any discussion of what was really troubling us.

Yet these same complaining soldiers could sustain severe wounds and the loss of close comrades with an amazing stolidity. I found that among the wounded, the screamers—those who cried out the most when hurt—were often not the most severely injured. Those who lay quite still or softly asked for water or a cigarette could slip away quietly from shock or blood loss.

The noisy ones often recovered completely, but while they were in full cry, they seriously upset the rest of the troop. Not only was such behavior considered unseemly, but it served to remind us of how fragile we were. Sometimes we would be tempted to put someone out of his misery, for his sake, we said, but what we really wanted was for him to shut up, for our sakes. So, in a curious way, we tended to shun the wounded, even if good friends, for fear that their bad luck would rub off.

While we were saddened and angered by the death of a comrade, we were also secretly elated to be alive and unwounded. Our fear of death was counterbalanced by our delight in not being one of his chosen.

When you go out on patrol, you rarely look up. You look deeply into the shaded valleys, the hidden turns, all the places where the ambushes lie. You always expect the cough of the 88's, the sound that makes your body twitch away from incoming mutilation. A soldier with a strong imagination is an unhappy one. You have to harden yourself, or go mad with the tension. Yet with all this, there is still a tumultuous joy when you return from a patrol, safe and unharmed.

That is why these few months or years at war are the vantage point from which one views and measures the rest of one's life. Despite the omnipresence of death, or perhaps because of it, one feels so alive. With all that terror and danger, there is also a thrill that unites us. You bond instantly to strangers who become comrades under fire. You never forget them, even if you never see them again. They remain in your mind forever, lithe and energetic, ever young.

Nix Nazi

After reading part of a fascinating book by Daniel J. Goldhagen entitled Hitler's *Willing Executioners: Ordinary Germans and the Holocaust,* I was reminded of my own experiences dealing with these same German *Volk* [people].

During World War II, in my role as a military interpreter under the aegis of a purported military genius named George S. Patten, I swept into Germany near the city of Trier, with the entire Third Army backing me up. It was there, long before we crossed the Rhine, that I first encountered and heard the phenomenon of Nix Nazi. Every German citizen I met, especially those with political or military connections, would immediately and vehemently exclaim to me, without preamble or prompting, "Nichts Nazi."

Initially, I thought this rubric was short for Vernichts Nazi, that is, the Nazis should be destroyed. But I soon realized that they had the chutzpah to announce defensively that, despite all appearances and the frequent newsreels of Germans at Hitler's pageants shouting themselves hoarse in admiration of the Nazi regime, they were Nichts Nazi—not Nazis.

They said that one had to go along to get along, but that deep down, they had sincerely detested the Brown Shirts and the Thousand Year Nazi Reich—which lasted only 13 years. American soldiers, with their tin ears for foreign anguages and tendency to simplify foreign words, soon corrupted this phrase into "Nix Nazi," which it remained until we left Germany.

The Germans, detecting from my accent that I was a Jew, were still most eager to be on my side, the winning side, and invariably buttressed their claim with another comment: *Ich war immer nicht politisch,* that is, "I was always non-political." This was absurd. It was as though one could waltz through 13 years of the Nazi madness, enter a university, be elected to political office, get a good job or apartment, obtain a ration book, or send a son to the army, without expressing a political opinion in favor of the regime.

They all participated in the Winter Hilfe, winter relief that provided warm clothing, often stolen from the Jews, to send to German soldiers trapped in Russia's snows. They all participated in political rallies, bought war bonds, put down deposit money for the soon-to-be-delivered people's car, the Volksvagon. They all did everything they could to show adulation and support for the divine Adolf, all the time being "non-political."

One would have to believe that they were sleepwalkers who never woke to notice that the synagogues were burning; that their Jewish and socialist neighbors were being beaten in the streets; that people were disappearing after a visit from the Gestapo. They eagerly bought, at fire sale prices, art treasures, jewels, furniture and clothing sold by their desperate neighbors eager to collect funds, so as to go elsewhere—anywhere.

They quickly took over houses and apartments, businesses and practices vacated by deported or fleeing Jewish neighbors and competitors. They saw nothing, they heard nothing, and they most definitely said nothing. Many actually denounced hidden Jews to the Gestapo to curry favor or gain some advantage. Since they had not been directly involved in hauling off the Jews or sending them to the gas chambers, euphemistically called "Resettlement in the East," their hands and their consciences were clean, they thought.

As part of my job, I would ride in the lead vehicle of our unit whenever we came to a small city or town where we might billet for a night or two. It was my task to find the *Burgermeister* or Mayor and duly inform him that we would need a certain number of houses for the battalion to use for headquarters, medical facilities, supply facilities and other activities. I would sternly tell him to get into my vehicle and I would point out the houses we would need. Never did a Burgermeister refuse or even protest.

Naturally, I would select the largest and best-kept houses for our purposes. However, I would assure him that we would not destroy or loot the houses we occupied and we would be moving on soon. Most of the time I was able to keep that promise.

I would command the Burgermeister to inform the unhappy householders that they had two hours in which to collect any personal belongings and valuables and to vacate the premises. "*Rause* [Get out]!" the soldiers who accompanied me would shout delightedly. What they lacked in linguistic ability, they made up for in enthusiasm.

Not once did any family demur or hesitate. Well-disciplined and trained from birth to accept orders from authority, the Germans obeyed without protest. Sometimes they would ask what things they could take. I would generously indicate that they could take anything they desired, including food and furniture, which we would not need.

Once I single-handedly cleared out an entire floor of a German military hospital to make room for our own wounded and not once did the doctors, administrators or the wounded officers and soldiers utter a word of protest, much less of defiance.

A curious thing would take place whenever we came to collect our Burgermeister. His wife and children would start to scream and a great commotion would take place. The words *geschossen* or *schiessen* [shot or shooting] would be heard frequently. The mayor always approached me obsequiously, white-lipped and trembling. He obviously thought that we would shoot him and I wondered at the apparent fear.

I know that the noisy arrival of my jeep or my preferred armored car, loaded with heavily-armed enemy soldiers, was not designed to soothe anyone. I was unconcerned about how they felt because I had a purpose in the theatrics. We wanted immediate compliance without the need to resort to cruelty or killings. As I swung off my vehicle, unshaven and with an unorthodox and illegal Tommy gun slung over one shoulder, I gave off a piratical impression that was frightening. But even after I indicated that we did not intend them any harm, even after we did not hit or curse them, the fear was still palpable. Each mayor was obviously terrified.

Only after I was briefly detached to interpret at what we thought was a large forced labor camp called Dachau, did I realize why they were so afraid. They knew! They knew who was in those freight cars and where those inhumanely packed trains were going. They knew what their destinations and their fates were.

They thought we knew and expected to be shot out of hand in retribution. But our ignorance stood between them and our revenge. The American soldiers were completely unaware of the Shoah, the Holocaust, and unaware of its magnitude, its fierce cruelty and brutality.

When we were finished with the mayor, we would often bring him home. We would whirl up to his front door and, as he stepped out of our vehicle, his family would greet him as though he had been released from the clutches of death. Embraces, kisses and tearful shouts of joy filled the air.

They knew. They all knew. Despite the voluminous denials, THEY ALL KNEW!

Later we forced the local citizenry, especially the elite, to walk through the newly liberated camps and see and smell what their god, Hitler, had wrought. They covered their noses and in tearful voices cried out their sorrow, their innocence and their ignorance of these ghastly proceedings. Enraged, I would often slap aside a handkerchief covering the delicate nose of an "innocent" and order him to breath deeply and *gedenk,* remember.

As the war ground down to a halt, my battalion found itself in a pretty resort town called Kochel am Kochel See in Upper Bavaria, not far from Berchtesgaden. There I was the sole authorized contact between the civilians and the American Army. Fraternizing was verboten for both sides, but the soldiers often managed to evade this directive and some women managed to get themselves pregnant.

Having seen what had taken place in the camps, I had little patience with the local populace and their attempts to ingratiate themselves with me. I gave my orders sternly, with much waving of weapons. These orders, including curfews and the relinquishing of all weapons, were obeyed promptly. I had to laugh when I noticed that among the piles of swords and pistols that were turned in, someone had put in a whole set of silverware under the impression that the cutlery might be considered weapons.

However, when the Germans discovered that the Amis, theAmericans, were not the Russians, who looted their homes and factories, raped their women and shot resisters out of hand, they regained their arrogance and soon began to come to me with complaints. This house was broken into by troops; soldiers were using fences for fire wood; chickens and geese were being stolen; girls were being propositioned; someone had made off with an entire inventory of French Chanel Number Five perfume, undoubtedly stolen and sent home by the victorious German troops four years earlier.

In short, they seemed to think that they had rights and had come to me to seek, nay demand, justice. Furious, I snatched up my Tommy gun and let loose a burst into the ceiling.

Raging, I informed them loudly that they had no rights except those I chose to grant them. I reminded them of the cruel Aktionen, sweeps of trained killers, of the ghettos and the infamous Vernichtungs Lagers, the extermination camps. They should be grateful that I was not permitting the hungry, wandering slave laborers and displaced persons to ravage and loot the town. There were no more complaints, but later I was told that some had the temerity to go to the Third Army headquarters in Munich to complain that they were being abused—by a Jew. They were tossed out.

The other Americans were delighted at my outburst, even though they understood not one word of my angry tirade. One soldier said, "It sounds much worse when you don't understand the language."

I was sorry that I could not put the whole town to the torch and shoot the whole town council. But by then, the early omens of the Cold War could be felt, and the need to get the German economy and infrastructure going again created a mad rush to de-Nazify the worse Nazis. Werner von Braun, who was questioned by me briefly and who thought we would shoot him because of the destruction caused by his terrible V2 rockets, was treated as an honored guest and later made head of our missile program. Nichts Nazi or not, he was too valuable in our impending conflict with the U.S.S.R. to discard or imprison.

My Adventures in a Convent

The title seems somewhat salacious, but my adventures were as pure as the driven snow.

Let us turn the clock back to May 1945 and the location to southern Bavaria. My unit, the 609th Tank Destroyer Battalion, part of the tenth Armored Division and the Third Army, was busy mopping up the scattered remnants of the Wehrmacht and penetrating the last redoubt of the Nazi army. The last redoubt proved to be an illusion and we found ourselves burdened by hundreds of uniformed soldiers, begging to taken captive in order to get food and medical care. We refused them and sent them to the rear to be cared for by the Military Police.

When the war finally ground to a halt in May, I found myself in a small resort town called Kochel Am Kochel See. It was a beautiful area, filled with pine forests, lakes, and small farms and topped off by the glistening, snow-capped peaks of the Bavarian Alps. Who would believe that so much evil could come from there?

Since I was the battalion interpreter and, under the strict, non-fraternization orders, the only person aside from the Colonel who was permitted to converse with the German civilians, I was, in effect, the Allied Military Government of the entire area.

My nerves were still frayed from the sights and smells of Dachau, the concentration camp that we had just liberated. I was furious with the people, especially those who assured me that they were "nicht Nazi" and knew nothing of the camps. Despite the obsequious attitude of most of the people, I knew we were not far from Munich, the cradle of the Nazi party, as well as Hitler's Berchtesgaden.

Not a person or a sack of potatoes or a cow could move on the local roads without a *passierschein* or permission form written by my office. Since the Colonel had other things to do, this was my responsibility. I had set up my office in the best inn in town. Every morning, a line of people appeared with requests for various things and I granted them. They were a sober and frightened people and very respectful. Each would greet me with the words *"Gruss Gott"* when entering my office.

I would become furious with a fat *Burgermeister,* or mayor, who demurred when I requisitioned his home for our troops or a ramrod S.S. officer who was not properly courteous and denied being an officer. Sometimes, for spite, I would deny a request and shriek at them in German. The other soldiers would stand around grinning. One said: "It sounds much worse when you don't understand the language."

It was an exciting time for me. So much power and authority at my age! The various army patrols would report to me and bring in various high-ranking prisoners for me to question. Among the daily catch were Werner von Braun, the rocket scientist; Baldur von Schirach, head of the Hitler Youth and Gauleiter of Vienna; General Baron von Haushoffer (developer of the Lebensraum theory) as well as S.S. generals. Even Prince von Hesse, a descendant of the prince who rented the Hessian soldiers to King George III of England to fight the American colonists, had to come to see me to get gasoline for his automobiles. As we got acquainted—although never friendly—he loaned me one of his cars, a massive Mercedes staff car. I could not steal enough gas for it, so I went back to the Prince and borrowed a small Opel that met my needs perfectly. I planned to spirit that car home to the U. S. but the army said that would be strictly verboten.

One day as I went out with one of the patrols, I noted a very large structure high on a hill and the patrol stopped so that I could inspect it. As I dismounted in front of this massive, castle-like fortress, some twenty or thirty nuns came out quietly. They were like the mature nuns in the movie *Lilies of the Field,* but obviously frightened by the appearance of so many armed men. They stood resignedly and obediently awaiting our orders.

I had no orders for them. We had not even known they were there or what they were doing. The Mother Superior, a sweet-faced woman of fifty who reminded me of my mother, conversed with me. I learned that the convent was operating a hospital for sick farmers and wounded German soldiers, as well as an orphanage for dozens of "wolf children," abandoned or lost offspring of forced laborers, as well as a small elementary school.

The children, who had fearfully been peeking out of the doorways and windows, began to come out and we had a long conversation. The children spoke every European language, including Polish, Dutch, French and Greek, but no English or Yiddish. So I would develop a chain. I would say something in German to a child that spoke German and Polish. He would talk to another child who spoke Polish, French, and Russian and he spoke to another that spoke Russian and Greek and so on down the line.

It was rare that we could not find an interpreter for each child. In such cases, one of the nuns would intercede. I thought I had come up with a brilliant new idea for communication, but I learned that the nuns had done this long before. But I liked teaching and decided to become a teacher after the war.

The children fascinated me because they were true survivors. They had roamed the forests and the city streets, stealing to stay alive. Later I joked that they could steal your shoes while you stood in them. I was told by the Mother Superior that she thought several of the children they had sheltered were *mischlings*, half-Jewish children. Whether true or not, she won my heart with that comment.

The nuns escorted me through the hospital where I noted a woeful lack of any medical supplies. I said I would try to bring some the following day. The Mother Superior asked if I could also bring some food for the children. I could see that she doubted that I would keep my promise.

I asked the Battalion Medical Officer, the only other Jew in the Battalion, for extra supplies and he complied graciously. I knew I would be rejected by the mess sergeant (mess sergeants are notorious for being tightfisted) when I asked for food, so I brought some trading goods: a Leica camera, a Luger pistol, an Iron Cross, and so on. The mess sergeant would then load my vehicle with all the supplies it could carry. These goods were more precious than gold at that time, especially the chocolate.

The following day, when I drove into the convent court yard, the usually silent nuns shouted with joy. There was a lot of excitement and many willing hands took the goods inside. The Mother Superior thanked me profusely and was clever enough not to inquire whether this could get me into trouble. I gallantly ignored the risk, even though I knew it was a distinct possibility. Every few days I would repeat the trip until it became a routine.

The children would line up in the courtyard as I approached

and sing songs from a variety of homelands. The nuns would sing haunting liturgical music. Even wounded German soldiers would sing *Ich Hat Einen Kamaraden*. It was peace on earth and I was Daddy Warbucks.

This idyllic situation was shattered when my unit received orders to move promptly to Le Havre to be shipped Japan for the invasion. I went up to the convent and told the Mother Superior the sad news. The following day would be my last supply run, so I asked the Mother Superior what was most important to her. She asked for anesthetics for those who required surgery.

I knew that I was in Nazi country, but these simple, good-hearted women did not seem to be tainted. They were just extraordinary people caught in the clash of ideologies and armies.

That last morning, I drove up the hill to the convent with a truckload of supplies: flour, canned meats, oil, sugar and medical supplies. I was startled to see that no one but the Mother Superior was there. But she pointed up the hill and I saw columns of children and nuns singing as they came down. Each one held a small or large can filled with wild strawberries, the tiniest and sweetest strawberries one could ever find. After presenting me with the many cans of fruit they had collected, the Mother Superior thanked me, in German of course. The nuns smiled and the children sang as they put down their fruit-laden cans at my feet.

I was very touched by the scene and by how much effort had gone into this gift, so I only kept one large can of fruit. As I drove off for the last time, the nuns waved, the children sang and shouted and tears rolled down my cheeks.

Letters from the War

I wrote these letters to my wife while I was stationed overseas during the war.

FEBRUARY 12, 1945, AT SEA ABOARD THE R.S.S. MAURETANIA

My Darling,

I have seen pictures of troopships, even worked on them, but you have to be on one before you can really appreciate what the word "packed" means. I cannot tell you how many G.I.s we have aboard but suffice it to say that every inch of space is at a premium.

I switched to pencil because it easier to write on the rolling deck. Considering my inexperience, I am really taking this trip in fine fettle. I spend the day clambering all over the ship, that is, any part that is not out of bounds. Some of the boys are not doing so well and it is quite understandable. But I haven't had an uneasy moment yet & I have been eating like a horse. This would be a wonderful trip in peacetime with you along. Gosh, I got my "sea legs" but it will take some time to get my "sea arm" so I can write more legibly.

My sleeping quarters consist of a rack for my equipment, a double innerspring super deluxe hammock. But it is not really bad. The guys are really taking it in their stride, with a surprising low rate of sea-sickness and a high rate of good humor & singing, during the daylight hours anyway.

Blackout on the ship means blackout & no foolin', for which I'm grateful. Some damn fool might endanger the whole ship.

I think the censor will let me say that this boat is a large one, but I guess I better stop there, else this letter will be all cut up.

Did you get my double letter from my last camp? Or those 3 records I had made? I tried to say as much as I could in them but remember that I was in front of a group of grinning soldiers and had no chance to prepare a script. In case I did not make it clear my darling, I love you. More later.

Been touring the deck. It really is crowded but everyone is so nice about it you don't mind so much. Everyone laughs at some of the situations. The lack of space causes the officers to share what little they have. The officers and men mingle in such a democratic way, no one salutes or sirs unless you are on duty, just too friendly.

Ahem, We have aboard CENSORED LINES not many but enough to add leaven to the doughy mass of males and put them on their good behavior.

Later. I am constantly being interrupted by soldiers just wandering about, stepping on my feet (I am sitting on the deck). This constant restless pacing betokens a mental poverty. If they aren't reading comics, they tramp about. I just stand at the rail and look out at the sea (darling, it is almost every color depending on the sun, a deep metallic blue, a frothy white & aqua-green, purple and all constantly shifting) and just dream of you and muse about the day I will return to you.

I am writing this in addition to "V" mail. Feeding such a multitude of men is quite a problem. I'm glad it's not mine. Chow lines are long but as nothing compared to the lines to the canteens. Since I've been aboard I have been in one once but the deck is too lovely to spend hours below waiting in line. Besides I was foresighted enough to be well stocked up before I got on board.

When we left that familiar port I wondered how long before another ship would bring us back, and how many of us. But I want you to know darling I am coming back to you. I wrote my last letter in a hurry so I wonder whether you were able to read it.

More later.

Love, Milton

.

Darling,

I guess I am about the only guy in my outfit that is writing, but I know how hard it is to wait for a letter that never comes. We think we know where we are going, latrine rumors, hypotheses, & guesses, but it is the first, number one rule of censorship that we do not reveal even those dubious bits of information.

Frankly I've tried to figure it out by trying to picture our course according to the sun's position. After the first day out I was so snafued up that I'm not even sure the sun rises in the east. Talking to other amateur navigators just added to the confusion.

I was looking at the waves creaming away from the bow. The most startlingly beautiful blues and greens thrust at the beholder for a fleeting moment. I wish you were with me, love, for it is a beautiful view and you could enjoy it with me. The ocean is far from a sterile mass of water. It is a wondrous, moody show of color, constantly displaying different shades of her multicolored cloak. We even saw a rainbow, a breath-taking arc from horizon to horizon. Surely a good omen.

Often when the wind & toss of the ship grow too strong we are restricted from the open decks, but I often slip out onto the highest deck and stand bareheaded & face thrust into the flying spray & wind. What quirk of my personality causes me to adopt these heroic defiant attitudes even though no audience is present? Do I use these affectations to prop up a weak personality or am I just a fresh air fiend? Perhaps it is an unconscious imitation of motion pictures like "Wuthering Heights" etc. with noble Byronic heroes defying the elements for love & glory, etc. Pure pish and tuffle eh? More later.

Just returned from a session with the prancing pasteboards (cards to you). I know you dislike my gambling and that being a consistent winner does not detract from the evil, but darling there is nothing else to do. I've read and roamed the ship & read again and time just seems petrified, so I play cards & time races along and the air is filled with an unhealthy excitement. So darling, don't be angry. I am a poor victim of my own weakness (My God! what a phony line!)

Am going down now to our unappetizing chow which these last few days has grown steadily worse. But since it can get even worse I'm going down now to see how bad it's gotten. Seriously, though, it will keep body and soul together even if my stomach must undergo titanic struggles to retain it.

I think of you constantly and darling, I love you so much. I want you to forget that nasty scene my last night home. I was all worked up so please remember our other moments together. We did have lovely times together, even if they were only fragmentary moments.

Take my love and don't worry about me.

Love,

Milton

P.S. We have a ship's show tonight. Anything will get a torrent of applause after these many days of inactivity. Love, M.

My Darling Wife,

Yes. Although I cannot discuss the devious route we used to get here, I am now in France. I know that with your penchant for neatness you will be pleased to know fairly definitely where I am. It must be annoying to have a valuable piece of property as a husband, just straying about. It is much simpler when he can be pinned down to someplace definite. Seriously though I know you were worried.

You notice I am numbering my letters in order to help you check whether they all arrive. Please number yours.

As usual I am safe and well and thriving on this life so don't worry about me.

Give my regards to everyone, keep in touch with my folks and remember I am coming back soon. Keep thinking it as soon and it will be.

I love you. Milton

SUNDAY, FEBRUARY 25, 1945, SOMEWHERE IN FRANCE

My Darling,

I miss you terribly. Even in the hustle and bustle of the last several weeks, I thought of you. I would have liked to have written you but the conditions on the train made writing impossible. We were terribly crowded, the old 40 Homme and 8 cheveaux cars are in operation. It was an exhausting trip of several days and nights. I saw so much devastation throughout my journey. It was terrifying and heartbreaking.

The poverty of the people touched me very deeply. I was at once contemptuous and ashamed by the begging of the people for candy and cigarettes. Ashamed that we had so much and they so little and ashamed to see my fellow man groveling

147

for a literal crust. And the children. The solemn wise big-eyed stares of the ragged children was enough to tear your heart out. I have to see one in leather-soled shoes yet. Wooden soles and all-wood "sabots" are the usual sight. No healthy young men are to be seen. In fact, the good black earth lays like a good woman with no one to make her fruitful, for most of the towns & villages, even those that escaped the pounding of Mars and the wanton destruction of the Germans, are almost completely deserted.

I never dreamed that I would ever see France, certainly never under such conditions. Everywhere you can see evidence of the frugality, traditional with the French, careful planting of trees, skillful use of every inch of the soil, the dung heaps. Every Frenchman has his haversack with a bottle of dubious wine and a long thin loaf of bread sticking out.

French money is still curious and novel to us. It is so unreal as yet, like children's stage money. We have to convert all of our American and English currency into Francs. That is to prevent our selling our dollars on the Black Market & adding to France's troubles with the rampant tendency towards inflation. The Army's policy on this score is helping the people a great deal by "pegging" the Franc.

I know that you want to know all about me. Well, I'm not at my final destination, but at one of the innumerable "staging" & distribution points. Our stay here is uncertain so no more on that. It is warm here, comparatively, for which I am grateful. A winter at the front would be a horrifying prospect. I'm grateful for the approaching summer.

I'm going to use air mail exclusively henceforth, having heard that "V" mail from these parts is not so fast. Use airmail yourself. I know that I will not be able to receive any mail from home for some time, but keep on writing. Maybe I'll soon light long enough to receive some.

I want to request 1—A good, not too pedantic, French dictionary. The latter is more important. 2—A good German grammar and dictionary. I have a good "Betz & Price" grammar at home so dig it up and send it along. Keep lightness in mind (weight) when sending anything over. 3—I request some "eats," leaving the choice to your inimitable taste and discretion.

Darling, did you receive the poem I wrote you from my last camp in the States or did the censor, fearing some code, tear it into shreds? If you haven't I'll send it along again. Give my love to my folks and tell them not to worry. I'm quite safe and well.

I love you my darling wife. I dream of the day we can be together again.

Your devoted husband, Milton.

P.S. I just wrote to Murray.

THURSDAY, MARCH 1, 1945, SOMEWHERE IN GERMANY

My Darling,

I've been moved so often, from one distribution point to another, I've had no opportunity to write you. At the moment Bert, the Cape Cod boy, Stuart and I, are sitting in an abandoned home in a village. It is a good solid house and we used some ingenuity to make it as cozy as a bug in a rug. Dry and warm, Boy what a pleasure! Amazing how important things like that can become. We were able to manage a warm shower yesterday and the boys were bubbling over with joy at the thrill of being clean.

I am permitted to say I am with Patton's 3rd Army, but not definitely assigned. The Germans left here fairly lately and some of the boys are wandering around collecting souvenirs. I've gotten a childish delight out of translating road signs and books that we found. Tell my dad that we passed, some time ago, a place called "Mackensen Kaserne" which gave me a peculiar turn. My father used to speak of places like that. He actually fought in Mackensen's Army on the Eastern Front in WW I.

As yet we have not been in any combat, or even close to it, but evidence of its impact on buildings, and homes, upon streets & sanitation are amply available.

I've dreamt of you, of the day we can be together. I miss you, my darling. Keep writing me. As yet, I have not been able to stay long enough to receive mail, but maybe soon I'll settle down. I wish I knew for certain what outfit or even what sort of an outfit I am going into.

The land in Germany is not perceptibly different from French soil. Rich, good soil and well-tended farms, but no one working them. Such a wanton waste of lives and property. Such fine vineyards and orchards just torn up and laid flat.

Am I glad we are not in those God dammed cattle cars with its terribly cramped sitting and sleeping accommodations. A real night's sleep on one of them is out of the question. If one person moves, a wave of discontent and muttering surges through the rest of the tangled mass of uneasily dozing occupants.

Here I am living where awhile before some Hitler Heilers lived. We cooked our "c" rations on our small stove. I was looking at some of the good china (we ate off of it today) and delicate silverware. Good stuff and in taste too, but I'm not in the least bit tempted to carry any off. I'm so loaded down now with with important items necessary to keep Mrs. Stier from being widowed, I can barely walk.

My helmet has an awful dent in it but it's not from an eighty-eight, just from dropping it off a truck.

I'm in good health, really. This open air and movement is good for me. Sleeping in windowless houses and open box cars is good for the complexion. I love you darling.

Your devoted husband,

Milton

MARCH 2, 1945, SOMEWHERE IN GERMANY

My Darling,

I have moved again. Just as I finished the letter I wrote you this morning, orders came to out again. In fact, I did not even mail it, but gave it to a friend to mail. I hope he did. My new address is on the envelope. Send all my mail here from now on. I am in the Third Army.

As usual I have taken a large room for my personal billet and rigged up a nice comfortable home for myself. It took a little bit of doing, cleaning a shattered mess is always work, but it gives you a real sense of satisfaction. This literary master-piece is being painfully pecked out on a German typewriter; the English letters are a mystery to me.

Well here I am up close to where the headlines are being made; this is a large city but it has suffered from every type of projectile we or the Germans could throw at it. Too bad I can't be more precise in telling you where I am at, but...

Right now I am very tired, so I'll cut off for now and end this muddled and incoherent mess.

Take my love,

Your devoted husband,

Milton

My Darling,

Oh Happy Day and Hallelujah at last I've received mail from home. Letters 1-4 and a Valentine's card as well as a letter from my dad. The last letter was written Feb 20th. A month is not bad lag considering.

You ask such a wealth of questions that I am at a loss to start answering. I have sort of answered most of your queries in my previous letters.

First, I left the States that Sat. night. I made those recordings despite the fact that I had been alerted and we were restricted to barracks.

As for now things are pretty good...

April in Paris

Late in March 1945, I was serving with my armored battalion in the German Karlsruhe-Pforzheim area when the monthly lottery for three-day passes for leave in Paris took place. The battalion of approximately 1,500 men received about 20 of these precious three-day passes each month, and everyone hoped to win one and be able to enjoy the pleasures of Paris. Just being out of the front lines was a tremendous benefit, even without the romantic attractions of Paris—the mythic, the alluring, exotic city featured in so many books and films.

The commanding officer was remarkable because, rather than giving out the passes at his own discretion, he held a public lottery, actually drawing the names of the lucky recipients from a helmet. I sprang for joy when I was one of the lucky ones to be selected. There was some grumbling because, as the interpreter, I was considered close to the colonel; I was in the battalion for a relatively short period; and I was one of the few Jews in the battalion. Therefore, I was considered unworthy of such good fortune.

Others, more pragmatic, did not bother to complain because the commanding officer would not consider reversing his selections. They decided to bribe me for my precious pass. Cameras, pistols and money were offered in exchange for my pass. One sergeant even offered me $500, a large sum when a private earned only $50 per month.

However, my pockets were already filled with French and Belgian francs, English pounds and U.S. dollars which I had won at the endless crap and card games that went on between combat missions. I seemed to have such an amazing ability to judge the laws of chance and probability that my fellow soldiers gave me large sums of money. The fact I was both Jewish and a winner seemed to create an aura of suspicion that did not cling to non-Jews who played cards well and were heavy winners.

So I blithely refused all of the tempting offers and ignored their muttered curses and anti-Semitic comments and walked away singing "April in Paris."

The next week, clutching our precious passports to freedom, the group going on leave mounted a ponderous six-by-six army truck and endured hours of a bone-rattling ride through the German and French countryside, retracing the route we had taken when fighting our way into Germany—Heidelberg, Mannheim, Trier, and so on. Many times we looked for places where we had bivouacked or had a fire-fight; where companions had been lost; or where something humorous had taken place. But we were all too tired and too excited by the prospect of Paris to devote much time or thought to this interesting exercise.

Finally, dirty, hungry and tired we arrived at the Red Cross facility in Paris. Set up near the Gare du Nord, it provided for front-line combat troops on leave. There we took hot showers (oh, blessed joy!), were fed a hot meal, and had our uniforms cleaned and pressed. While we waited, some soldiers used the time to try to teach me the intricacies of blackjack. This ultimately cost them about $150, which I later spent on perfumes and other gifts to send home.

Then we all swarmed out to see and enjoy the vaunted glories of Paris. Most ignored the grand sweep of the Champs

Elysees and raced off to sample the charms and wares of Place Pigalle (called Pig Alley by the American troops), the notorious red-light district. I went along, not because I was interested, but because one had to tell one's comrades all about it when you returned. All of the soldiers had come prepared with trading goods, items that the deprived French population was panting for, such as cigarettes and soap, free to Americans and worth more than one dollar on the black market. Chocolate was often used for direct barter for sexual favors, with the immortal phrase, "Voulez vous Hershey bar?" or "Do you want a Hershey bar?"

The harsh, painted faces, the heated conversations, the noisy haggling and sordid surroundings made it into a most unpalatable scene. With enough data on which to build a fine series of "eat your heart out" lies, I was able to slip off and tour Paris alone.

There I was, wandering Paris on a lovely April day, well fed and full of money, so I went on a tourist binge. I rented a charcoal-powered taxi (as they had no petrol) and roamed the city, from Montmartre and Sacre Coeur to the Eiffel Tower, wherever my eyes led me.

I wandered into an ornate Algerian or Moroccan synagogue where I understood nothing of the service, but I was fascinated by the habit of each worshipper kissing the tips of his fingers and bowing towards the ark as they entered the or left the sanctuary.

It is too bad that I did not have the courage to start a conversation with the worshippers. I might have learned something about North African Jewish rituals, which were as remote to me those of Druids.

I looked at the stylish, attractive women, even under the severe deprivation of wartime conditions, with their upswept hairstyles, many with a dyed white streak, as they went clacking across the streets in their wooden clogs. Leather was impossible to obtain. I had never eaten real French bread before and I devoured the crusty flavorsome baguettes and greedily ate the warm roasted chestnuts offered by the vendors near the Tuilleries and the Louvre.

It was curious. The light of the city seemed strangely luminescent. Perhaps it was because I was happy and tension-free. I could smile at the black marketers who would sidle up to me to buy anything I had—soap, cigarettes, chocolate, dollars. They were desperate men with bad teeth, ill-fed and ill-clothed.

Remember, this was just before I visited Dachau and the whole horror of the Final Solution became common knowledge. So, apologetically, I must say that the French made a worse impression on me that the German citizenry. The latter were much cleaner, more orderly and industrious. Within a few weeks after our armies had shattered the city of Kaiserlautern, the Germans had cleaned up the mess and had collected and stacked usable bricks and cobblestones for future use. In France, the wreckage of fighting from almost a year earlier was still in evidence, except where American G.I.s had cut roadways through the rubble for the Red Ball Express, the supply-carrying truck convoys.

The furtive looks, the generally rapacious attitude toward the "rich" Americans who had liberated them, turned me off on the French. Our battalion had a brief assignment to assist LeClerc's or DeTassigny's armored forces to reach Paris the previous year. We found the French to be impossible—arrogant, lazy and inefficient. We constantly had to repair their vehicles because they were so indifferent to common maintenance procedures. To add to that, we were resentful that the Third Army was restrained so that the French could have the honor of entering and "liberating" Paris first. With the help of American mechanics, they were able to lurch into some semblance of a victory parade. I had missed Paris that time and now I savored it even more fully.

Paris is a peculiar city in that streets constantly change their names every few squares. Few streets cross each other at right angles, so that it is an easy city in which to get lost—a maze without readable street signs.

I was depressed at the sight of old men scrounging in the gutters for cigarette butts discarded by the rich Americans, but I enjoyed the flower-seller carts piled high with glorious, colorful flowers. Since we had no such displays in New York, I realized that the City of Light had some truly civilized touches. The streets were swarming with almost every conceivable uniform in the world. Most of the Allied armies were represented, and the streets flickered with the constant saluting of officers.

Then the news came—the Germans were surrendering! An armistice was being declared for tomorrow! Such rumors had swept through Paris and the American Army several times in the previous weeks. It was obvious from the speed of our advance, more than 25 miles on some days, that the Germans were exhausted. In one week in March we had advanced a greater distance than the Allied armies did in four years of the ghastly trench warfare of World War I.

So it was clear that peace was imminent, now that the Battle of the Bulge had destroyed the last major forces of the Nazis and we were meeting the Russians at the Elbe.

Therefore we thought this armistice of April 2nd was real, that war was over and this day would be entered into the history textbooks and celebrated in the future. Everyone was ecstatic. Strangers hugged and kissed each other. People stood about shouting with joy. I even hugged and kissed French men. Then I bought a whole cart of flowers and flagged down an American jeep loaded with soldiers. We hooked the cart to the jeep and raced up and down the various boulevards screaming, *"La guerre est finie!"* while hurling flowers at the smiling passersby. The people laughed and shouted and threw the flowers back at us. A delirious flower fight took place and the street looked like a snowfall of petals.

I asked one of the others, "Do you think I have to go back? Now that it is peace can't I just stay in Paris until they ship me home?"

His brilliant reply was, "I don't know, feller."

I really knew that the Army had its own way of doing things and that I would have to return to my outfit. I raced back to the staging area under the misapprehension that the earlier I returned to my unit, the sooner I would be discharged and sent home.

There I learned that that I was wrong. There was no armistice! The peace was just another in a series of false alarms. The Germans were still fighting stubbornly and hard, and our troops, especially the armored forces, were taking heavy casualties. What bad luck! With peace so close, to buy the farm at that stage seemed too terrible to contemplate.

So, tired, depressed and fearful, I went home to my outfit. Since the unit had pressed even deeper into Germany in my absence, it took longer to catch up with them. Finally, I met them between Ulm and Augsberg, on the way to Munich.

There I learned that my pass had truly been a lucky ticket. My tank had fallen through a weakened bridge over the deep, swift-flowing Danube near Ulm. Only one member of the crew had avoided drowning. He was in such sad shape that he was assigned to clerical duties the rest of the campaign.

We had been holed by German 88 cannons and had had vehicles burned, but who would dream that one could drown in a tank? It was ironic that the sergeant who had offered me $500 was a casualty.

I was assigned to another tank crew, but since we were strangers they viewed me with indifference and fear. I was a Jonah who survived the demise of his whole tank crew. My assignment was brief, however, because I was ordered to serve as an interpreter of a vast labor camp we had just liberated near Munich.

What our army stumbled into was Dachau, and none of us were prepared for what we were to see. Other units had already spread out in the camp when I arrived, but even then the scene was indescribable. Bodies were being bulldozed into vast pits serving as mass graves. I was severely shaken by the sight of emaciated skeletons smiling at me and then falling over dead. The dying was continuing even as we tried to feed and save them. When I addressed them in Yiddish, some seemed to gain some strength and the will to live. The idea of an armed Jewish soldier coming to rescue them was both unbelievable and uplifting to them. The story of those days has been told and retold so many times that I cannot dwell on it without pain and guilt. How could I have been so unaware of this horror?

What struck me most was the unbelievable stench. Excrement, vomit, mounds of corpses, unwashed bodies, filthy straw beds, all mingled into an intolerable assault on the nostrils. I felt guilty, yet grateful, when I was sent back to my combat unit. I could not stand those terrible, staring eyes for another day.

I rejoined my battalion in an area south of Munich near Garmisch-Partenkirchen, on the way to Berchtesgaden. There we endured vicious ambushes by the retreating Wehrmacht troops and absurdly tragic assaults by youngsters of the Volksturm whom we killed when they tried to blow up our tanks with bazookas.

We also fought the first fighter jet aircraft in the world. One morning we were bombed by three planes—without propellers! On the first bombing pass, we were so astonished we just looked at them with mouths agape, as they flew by at unbelievable speeds. At the next pass, I leaped up onto my tank and fired our 50 caliber machine gun directly into the front of one of the strange, sleek aircraft. And I shot it down! Of course, every other unit in the area was also firing at the same few planes and everyone claimed that he had shot it down. But I really know the truth—it was I. I was a non-flying ace but, unfortunately, unrecognized as such.

As the collapse of the German forces became more imminent, we could not send out a patrol or a supply convoy without attracting hordes of German soldiers eager to surrender so that they would be fed. At one point, we refused to accept surrenders because the numbers curtailed our mobility. We told them to walk to the rear, where the POW camps were being set up. So the once powerful German Army stood along the roadside looking woeful as we didn't even want them as prisoners. After Dachau, I was unconcerned that some of the prisoners were shot while trying to escape while being marched back to POW camps.

Finally, the real armistice took place: VE Day, May 7th. Soldiers went wild—bullets, shells and rockets were all shot off into the sky to celebrate the glorious occasion. We had survived.

I sincerely hope that no one was killed by the extravaganza of deadly fireworks that took place. Now it was a fact. "La guerre est finie," and we all waited eagerly to be sent home.

The Army established a point system, where each month overseas, each campaign ribbon, each medal earned, would be worth so many points toward early shipment home and demobilization. About 80 points seemed to be the magic number for early release.

We were unlucky as our battalion was not designated to be disbanded. We were still needed for the future invasion of Japan. A battle-hardened armored group like ours would be invaluable to such a difficult assault. So, after two interesting months serving as the "governor" of Kochel in Ober Bayem, I was ordered with my outfit to return to France to embark for the States. There we would be reequipped and sent to a Pacific port for deployment to Okinawa for the invasion of the home islands of Japan.

Since I was the interpreter for the unit, the Army continued my designation. It thoughtfully sent me a Japanese dictionary and a grammar book and asked that I spend the travel time brushing up my linguistic skills in that language so that I would be fluent when I arrived. I can proudly say that after endless hours of poring over the books, I learned not one single word to add to my already extensive vocabulary, which consisted of "Banzai," "Sayonara," and "Kamikazi." I later learned more Japanese from watching *Shogun* than I did reading those cryptic Japanese symbols and letters.

We left Le Havre in August, and when we arrived in New York City in September, we were greeted with the joyous news that VJ Day had occurred. The Japanese had surrendered and the dreaded amphibious invasion would not take place. We were not needed! Embarrassed by our presence, the Army granted us 45-day leaves to go home. So without points, without the lengthy processing, we had lucked out and were among the first troops to come home from the European theater.

I decided that since I was already in New York, I would surprise my wife. I raced to her parents' home, where she was living while I was saving the world. I opened the door and stood there with my duffle bag over my shoulder, just like all of those Norman Rockwell paintings. She was sitting at the dinner table, a fork suspended in front of her mouth, and in total surprise and disbelief, she cried out the immortal phrase, "What are you doing here?"

Ah well, it wasn't a bad war, as wars go.

Photographs

Top, Left: My younger brother Murray (left), my sister Gladys (center), and me (right), 1929 or 1930, in Brooklyn. We all look glum because we had each just gotten a whack from my father for fidgeting.

Top, Right: My parents, Molly and Josef Stier, dressed for a family wedding.

Bottom: Murray, Gladys and myself in 1970

After graduation from DeWitt Clinton High School at 16, standing on the bridge over 174th Street in the Bronx

Dressed as an usher for a friend's wedding in 1939, at age 20. This was my "Ronald Coleman" period

My girlfriend Greta, an aspiring actress, in 1940

Above: At 21, showing off my riding outfit on the roof of our apartment building

Opposite, Top: With my horse Cheyenne, in 1941, at the Split Rock Academy in the Bronx where I took weekly riding lessons

Oppositre, Bottom: The girlfriend who inspired the story "The Fiddle"

Opposite: Selma visiting me at the army base in Louisville, Kentucky, in 1944. This visit was the basis of the story, "Weekend Pass."

Above: This photo was taken in 1945 just before Selma and I got married and I was sent overseas

Opposite: In front of my tank, April, 1945

This page, Top: In front of the Kochel town hall in the car borrowed from Prince von Hesse, May, 1945

This page, Bottom: Petitioners in Kochel lining up to see me, May, 1945

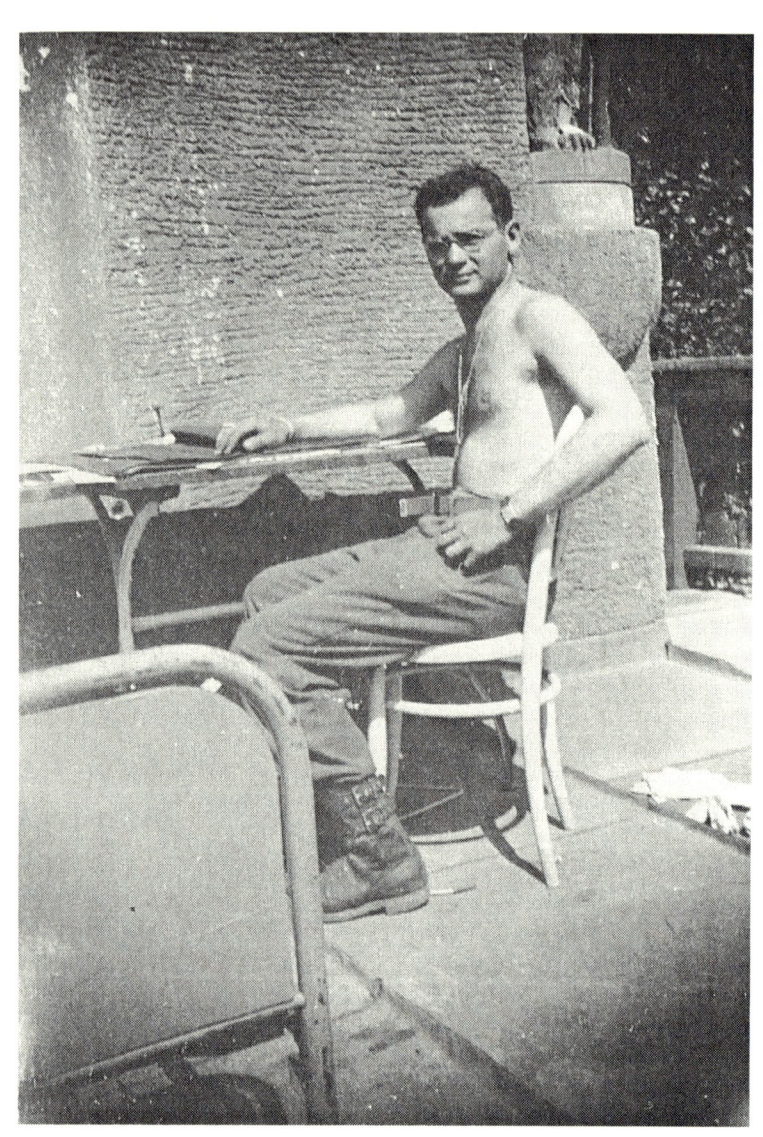

Opposite: At the Hotel Kochel, writing home, June 1945

This page, Top: Camp Brydon Lake, where I was a camp director from 1948 to 1962

This page, Bottom: My sister-in-law Helen is on the bottom left, with her husband Jerry above, holding their son, Arnie. My wife Selma is on the bottom right, with me above, holding our daughter, Emily. This was in 1948, at the camp, as we were working to set it up.

Top: Friends invited up to the camp on the weekend of Memorial Day, to help set up. I am top left, with my wife Selma just below me. Her parents, Lee and Blanche, are below her in the center. Blanche holds our daughter, Emily. My brother-in-law Jerry is next to Blanche, holding his son, Arnie. Helen, Jerry's wife and Selma's sister, is kneeling in the front center, below her parents.

Left: Friends invited up to the camp on Labor Day weekend, 1947, to help set up. Bottom left is my wife's mother, Blanche, with Selma second from the left. Helen is second from the right. My father-in-law Lee is top left, with me standing next to him. Jerry is second from the right.

Top: From left to right: Milton, Emily, Selma, Helen holding new-born Joanne, Arnold and Jerry. Camp Brydon Lake, 1950

Bottom: Jerry and I at camp singing *We've Got Each Other*

Ice-skating at Grossingers with my wife-to-be, Selma, whom I had just met. February, 1944.

Above: My daughter Emily's wedding in 1968. From left: My father-and mother-in-law, Lee and Blanche, my son Gordon, me, Selma, Emily and her husband George, my parents, Molly and Josef.

Left: My mother, Molly, holds my first grandchild, Joshua, as my daughter Emily and I stand behind her, in 1979. My mother died later that year.

My granddaughter Rebecca's bat mitzvah, in 1995 From left to right, my wife's cousins, Bill and Rae Marel, my grandson Joshua, kneeling, with my niece Joanne above him with her mother, Helen, and my son Gordon above Joanne. Rebecca is in the center in white, with her parents, George and Emily, behind her. Selma and I are in the front row next to Rebecca, with my sister Gladys and my brother Murray behind us. His wife, my sister-in-law Betty, stands next to me.

My daugher-in-law Beth, my grandchild Jessica, and my son, Gordon.

For Dr. Milton Stien,
Best Wishes —
Rosalynn Carter

This page: I was invited to the White House to meet Rosalynn Carter in 1977

Opposite: Me at age 38 just after my promotion to Assistant Principal, in 1957

Camp Days

Fear of Fire: The Early Years

All through my experiences as a summer camp director I was overcome by fear, fear that my charges would come to harm while I was responsible for them. This fear haunted me at all times, so I could rarely sleep through a night. Often I was certain that the bunks were on fire.

So I would find myself at two a.m., wandering about the campgrounds, visiting the bunks, looking for the fire that would endanger the campers. Usually I would get by on moonlight alone, but on truly dark nights I would use a flashlight. I probably frightened some sleepless boy or girl as my ghostly lamp moved about.

In all of the years at camp, we never had a fire in any of the bunks, though we had a small but dangerous one in the kitchen. That did not stop my nightmares. I still walked about, the spirit of protection incarnate. (Later, as a junior high school principal, I also had the same worries about my school and my pupils.) I never walked into the girls' bunks, after one time when I found that some girls slept in a rather embarrassingly uncovered way. I visited the boys' bunks often and borrowed some interesting comic books. I made certain to return them the following night, but sometimes I delivered the comic to the wrong bunk. Since I had to be in the kitchen by six AM, ready for a long and arduous day's work, it is remarkable that I was never late, given my nocturnal activities.

Wandering about at night was hazardous, which is why we were so hard on campers who went on midnight raids to other bunks (usually to those of the opposite sex). Once, while skirting a newly built bunk, I stepped into a deep hole left by the builders for a foundation and smashed my left hip. I am grateful that the bone was not displaced, but for the last forty years I have had pain in that joint and it has been getting worse in the last decade. It is an unhappy memento of the camp.

But I have other happier reminders of those days. My niece asked me to write down my memories and I find that each image recalls another. Each memory quickly slides into another and I lose track of what happened when. The early days, however, stand out clearly.

How we started the camp was interesting. Jerry, my brother-in-law, always wanted to be a director of a sleep-away camp. He had a friend in Rockaway who had invested in a piece of property on which he and a partner were building a summer camp. Since the project was now costing more than anticipated, he wanted to sell out for $6,000. This was sometime in 1947. I had no interest in the camp, as it was totally out of my experience, but my mother-in-law Blanche took me aside and said, "Jerry has no business experience but you do." (I had been the owner of two successful meat shops and a foreman at General Motors.) "Help him start the camp and after a year or so you can leave." I rather casually agreed and it turned out to be a 15-year commitment.

Jerry had no money and I had just gone bankrupt with my plastic toy factory, so we turned to other sources: my father-in-law Lee, and later my father and a bank. Lee was willing, reluctantly, to lend us $4,000. I borrowed another $4,000 from my father and with this meager capital we bought half of the project. We also inherited a partner, another health education teacher like Jerry and a uniquely stupid man. He had no talents whatsoever to offer the camp. (We could not stand him, so we bought him out the second year.) We persuaded a local bank in upstate New York to advance us $17,000. (I never understood why we settled on such a peculiar amount.) With this money and a vast amount of sweat equity, we worked to get the camp ready for its first season.

My wife Selma and I and Jerry and his wife Helen, Selma's sister, plus our two infants, Emily and Arnie, all lived in the old farmhouse, sharing a large room, without heat. The head counselors, the doctor and his wife, and the other senior staff lived upstairs, with about ten people sharing a tiny bathroom.

The downstairs of the vast barn was converted into a dining room and kitchen, while the upstairs hayloft became a recreation hall, or rec hall, and an arts and crafts shop. This building was supposed to be temporary, but we never took it down, although we did move the arts and crafts shop to a separate building. In fact, I think it still stands, unchanged.

We had to build a new road to the camp, less steep than the main one, Cabin Hill Road, which was an unpaved dirt road that passed the camp property. We had to bring in more electricity and an essential utility—a telephone line. No parent would send a child to a camp without some way of calling us. For years we struggled with a single line into the camp and it created a lot of distress. Helen was the guardian of the phone and allocated the time for campers and counselors to use it. Later we put in a pay phone and that took some of the burden off us.

We had to drill for a consistent and plentiful water supply and create a drain field so that the wastewater would be treated before it was released into the lake. Since we knew absolutely nothing about such details, we had to make things up as we went along or depend on our neighbors or hired hands to teach us our trade.

The camp was operated in a frugal shoestring fashion and we never hired anyone to do any job we thought we could do ourselves. Since Jerry had camping experience, was a gym teacher and had enrolled a majority of the campers, he would be the "outside" camp director. Helen had some bookkeeping experience, so she became the chief financial officer and was in charge of the guesthouse. Since I had butcher experience, I was put in charge of all of the scut work at the camp: the kitchen and dining room, maintenance and repairs, the water supply and the sewer system. Selma, with her dietitian experience, was put in charge of purchasing food, planning menus and harassing the kitchen help and the camper-waiters.

Helen also drove the camp station wagon to the horseback riding stable until she drove off the road into the Delaware River. Although the car, filled with girls, turned over several times and landed in the river upside down, no one was seriously injured. After that, Selma was the camp's designated driver, once she learned how to drive a stick shift car. She took all of the children to visits to the hospital for x-rays and similar errands.

Jerry was assisted by two head counselors, one for the girls and one for the boys, a waterfront man, an arts and crafts counselor, plus ultimately, some 20 to 40 counselors.

I was assisted by Mr. Anderson, the immortal Norwegian handy man, plus a chef, a baker, several dishwashers, salad girls and hordes of inept camper-waiters. Since the kitchen help tended to be unreliable, Selma and I were often called upon to substitute for all of the above. After a few such events, I became a fairly competent cook, baker and dishwasher. One terrible week with no dishwashers, Selma and I worked on the pots, pans and dishes until 11 at night. Despite this the kitchen was open and food was prepared every meal during every camp season. But it cost us something in health.

With money scarce, we bought everything second-hand. I got an ancient walk-in refrigerator for $600. We cooked our meals the first season on army gasoline-fired army field kitchens. Not only were they inefficient, as they would go out in the middle of a meal, they were downright dangerous and we had several near explosions or fires. The second year I refused to work with them, so we reluctantly bought three large restaurant stoves.

The beds and mattresses were all army surplus and nothing matched. The first mattresses were thin pads and caused many complaints. We later replaced them. Buying cheap always turned out to be expensive because we had to buy things twice. I bought most of our stuff at auctions so nothing came from the same place. Later, as we became established, we bought new equipment such as canoes, sunfish sailboats, mowers, and so on.

In the dining room, the tables were Navy surplus and heavy enough to cause a hernia if you moved them. The crockery was about as mixed up as possible and the chairs were totally mismatched. There was not a matched pair in the entire room. We never replaced the chairs, but we got rid of the heavy Navy benches, which had a bad habit of tipping over and hitting the campers' feet. I had become a *maven,* an expert, on purchasing things in the Bowery. As we discovered we needed something, I would buy it: pitchers, ladles, knives, large pots, baking pans, silverware, and on and on. The counselors stole the silverware to use in the bunks. As I look back, we were foolish; we did not feed them enough and they tended to steal food to balance the equation.

For on-camp chores we had a rickety blue van called the Blue Goose that had no starter motor. So we always parked it on a slope, hoping that by releasing the brake the motor would kick in. Sometimes that worked and sometimes it didn't.

Before the summer started, we had to make arrangements with various Delaware County vendors for horses to ride, fruit, vegetables, bread, milk, cream, butter, ice cream, and so on. We discovered how essential this was after we ran out of supplies several times. Selma was skilled at tracking down fresh corn and other staples. In addition to this, from mid-March on we went up to the camp every weekend to see how the workers were repairing winter damage and to prepare the camp for the opening. Later in the spring, I helped pretty up the place by planting flowers on the main lawn and around the flagpole.

On Memorial Day weekend of the first few years we would bring our wives and children up to the camp, so that while Jerry and I were teaching, Selma and Helen could spend the month of June bossing the workers to be certain that the camp was ready. We would often infuriate them when we came up on weekends and noted that there was very little visible progress for the week.

How we had the courage, and how our wives stood it, I will never understand. There they were, with infants, spending all week in an unheated house (the temperature could drop sharply in the mountains), in a desolate, alien area and expected to work like slaves with no real appreciation from their husbands. They would oversee the painting, the repairs, the placement of the trunks in the specific bunks, the storage of the canned goods and all of the multitudinous details of establishing a small town.

Sometimes we lost friends while building the camp. We would ask acquaintances, "Would you care to spend the weekend at our summer place?" They frequently agreed. When we got them up there, they were put to work painting the bunks or the barn, digging sewer lines, moving trunks and other delightful sports. My wife's youngest sister, Evy, still recalled with anger 50 years later how we had lured her and her husband up to the camp to paint the barn. The rough splintered boards of the barn could snatch a paintbrush bald in ten strokes and could swallow a gallon of paint without changing color. After a while we gave up and let it lay in its gray coat.

How we survived that first learning year I will never know. In fact we almost didn't. During the first season, on the 4th of July we had a fearful hailstorm that knocked out our electricity, which stopped our water supply and the chlorinator. Just then the health inspector visited us and announced that we were now a health hazard and had to be shut down. On the verge of hysteria, we pleaded for a day or two of grace. He eventually agreed and we made repairs and were back in business.

But we paid a toll. After the first season started, both Jerry and I became very ill from exhaustion, colds and probably the flu. We ended up in the infirmary. Actually we were the first patients housed there. As we lay there, we looked at each other and asked, "Who is running the camp while are here?" Knowing the answer, we got up, got dressed and against the advice of the doctor, went back to work. We simply got well because there was no alternative and we were young and strong.

We discovered once the first season got started that it was not only campers and counselors who required our attention, but parents as well. Weekends were especially hectic times. As camp directors, we had to be in six places at once because the parents were there. These keen and distrustful observers made us very cautious; we had to be careful, prompt, polite and sympathetic to complaints. Sometimes I was too tired to be a good example of any of these virtues.

Every Saturday night the campers and counselors put on some show, mostly for the benefit of the visiting parents who were eager to see their shy, unattractive and untalented offspring blossom into a well-poised talented star. After all, they were paying these outrageous camp fees, so they were "entitled." When the show was over, we offered each child a smile and a piece of fruit as they exited the rec hall. The children accepted the fruit but were not so receptive to the smiles.

Another feature that became a tradition was that the camp directors, spouses and head counselors, no matter how tired, would socialize with the guests, giving us an opportunity to praise their child's accomplishments at our wonderful camp and delicately hint about early enrollment for the next season. One burdensome task was preparing coffee and cake for the guests before they would call it a night. By evolution, this task was delegated to Helen. She would leave a bit early to get the coffee going in the directors' cottage (or later at the guest house lounge) and we would all join her.

Despite the command performance aspects of this chore, there were times when we had a lot of fun. Most of the parents were older than we were, but they enjoyed entering into the spirit of the camp. I would tell jokes and stories and Selma would lead off with some folk dancing. Many of the parents were excellent ballroom dancers, so we provided the music and all had a good time.

That first summer, we had managed to build three girls' bunks and three boys' bunk, able to house some 60 campers.

We had set our fee at the low end of the camping scale: $425 for the entire eight-week season and $375 for a second child in the family, plus $15 for canteen expenses. The parents were expected to tip the counselors and the waiters. (Many often stiffed our staff.)

Our initial contingent for the first season of 1948 consisted of 45 campers, so you can see that the total income was meager. The first few years, all we took home was $200 each from the coke machine. None of us were paid for our Herculean efforts. (Incidentally, one reason I became a teacher was because I could not hold another job and expect that they would release me every summer to run my camp.)

Each year we used our profits, miniscule as they were, plus money we had earned as teachers to build another bunk. Would you believe that I was the designated bunk architect? I would plan the size and shape of each new bunk and decide where the toilets, the beds and the windows should go—without knowing what I was doing. Somehow, it worked out. We ended up ultimately having enough bunks to house 120 to 150 campers at the munificent fee of $600 to $800 a camper.

The camp was central to our lives. Nothing could interfere with the running of the camp. For the first years, except for purchases or repairs, we never left the campgrounds. Even when Emily become seriously ill the first year, we brought in a burly farm woman to care for her because we could not spare the time away from our duties to take her to a doctor. Going to the movies was a luxury of our later years and we never went together

As it turned out, the horrors and errors of the first year made us more knowledgeable for the following years. We were too stupid to visit a well-run camp and copy what we saw, so we muddled through ourselves, with each year having its triumphs and tragedies. And everything I ever learned, from making 300 pancakes in one hour, to cleaning out a grease trap, to repairing shingles, was of use later in my career as a supervisor of schools. We all learned on the job and we got better as we went along.

The Indians: Counselors and Waiters

Jerry hired all of the counselors and in the first years he did remarkably well considering that we paid very little. I always thought of them as very young, since they were all between 18 and 21 years old, but now I realize that when I started as a director with no camp experience I myself was only 27, and Jerry just two years older. Yet we thought of ourselves as the elders and even when we had the time, we rarely socialized with them.

Most counselors disliked me because I was the Captain Bligh of our ship. While Jerry hired them, he never could bring himself to fire anyone. That task was always left to me and I had to put on my sternest face and escort them to town to take the bus home. Fortunately that happened infrequently, at least in the beginning, when it was almost impossible to replace a counselor. In later years we encountered drug users and pedophiles, but only rarely.

I learned almost all of my limited camp craft from the counselors. They taught me all about talent shows, color war, camp sings and camp dramatics, campfire ceremonies, songs and cookouts. I was always amazed at their exuberance, their creativity and their sheer enthusiasm, all of which evoked great reactions from the campers during Color War and the Camp Sing. (Color War divided the camp into two groups, the Blues and the Grays, who competed in athletics; the Camp Sing pitted the girls against the boys in performing parody songs, based on a theme such as Cowboys versus Indians.)

The counselors could whip up a musical, make and paint the sets, and rehearse their bunks in a week—all without any compensation except the sheer joy of being alive. I look back with great pleasure at the wonderful shows they produced and how much they added to the camp spirit. I still find myself singing some of the silly but happy songs they made up. "Itchy scratchy itchy scratchy, talcum powder" runs through my mind even now. And they put on wonderful full musicals with the campers: *South Pacific, I'd Rather Be Right, The King and I.* Their annual counselors' show was always a delight, even when they poked fun at Jerry and me. They often completed each project with no help from the bosses.

I recall how they once dressed the waiters as Iroquois warriors and then "raided" the campfire ceremony, to the shrieking delight of the girls. Sometimes Jerry and I got into the act, singing *We've Got Each Other.* One night I played the part of a swami, dressed in a turban, painted beard, and a large diaper and told each camper his fortune—with some humorous license. The younger campers were not fooled. They kept calling out that I was not an Indian fakir, but only Uncle Milton.

(For some reason, all camp directors were called "Uncle" and that put my daughter in a bind. She could not, like her bunkmates, call me "Uncle Milton" because my children never called me by my first name. So she compromised by calling me "Uncle Daddy." My niece tells me that she would solemnly inform her new bunkmates each year that Uncle Milton really was her uncle, but Uncle Jerry was her dad.)

I remember another way that I tried to amuse the campers. Every morning we would all meet at the flagpole to start the day with the Pledge of Allegiance and announcements from Jerry and myself. At some point I began to wear a different hat each morning: a French beret, a sombrero, an Indian headress. By the end of our camp years, I had accumulated a huge collection of hats, and my niece still makes a point of buying me one whenever she travels abroad.

The Seven Stripe idea was suggested by one of the early head counselors. Each stripe was a different color and represented a different virtue, such as sportsmanship, athletic skills, cleanliness, table manners, punctuality and so on. (My daughter tells me that she and her cousins still challenge each other to name all seven stripes and their colors and corresponding virtues.) Campers could be awarded one each week at a Friday night ceremony, after the religious service. (As this was a Jewish camp, with kosher style meals, we held Sabbath services on Friday night and Saturday morning.) If a camper received all seven, he was awarded a Seven Striper Patch to be sewn on a shirt or a pair of shorts. At the end of the season each such camper was honored at a special camp ceremony. Many children proudly wore them year after year. I often felt that Emily and Arnie and later Joanne, Helen and Jerry's younger child, were penalized by the counselors and denied stripes because the counselors resented the management, but I simply could not demand that my child be honored.

(I did ultimately talk to the counselors, asking that our children not be penalize. My niece remembers this differently. A counselor once told her that the directors said not to give their children seven stripes, even if they deserved them, for fear it would seem like favoritism.)

While we were older than most of the counselors, the elite counselors—the head counselors, arts and crafts counselor, the waterfront man, and so on—were older than we were and had immeasurably more experience. We listened to their suggestions and learned from them, but we were not in awe of them and gave orders that we expected to be obeyed. One head counselor, who brought us many new campers, was much older than we and had an overbearing manner to go with his broad experience. He insisted that not only was his daughter to be a free camper and his wife a guest, but his mother was also to be a guest. I faced him down and refused. When he threatened to quit, I said, "Okay," and he backed down. I warned Jerry that the following season we could not have him back because he thought he had us over a barrel. So we hired Leo Cooper, a wonderful warm, energetic and young head counselor.

One year, we hired a young female doctor, a most attractive blond woman who spent all of her free time reading medical books. At the end of the season we discovered, to our horror, that she was a fake. She had been a nurse briefly, had no real doctor's license and was carrying false papers. Now we knew why she was reading the books; she was looking for clues to diagnose the campers! We were caught in a cleft stick. To denounce her would evoke a flood of lawsuits. Since no one had been seriously ill or injured that year and everyone seemed satisfied with her medical care, we shut up and prayed that no one would learn of it. No one did. I destroyed her false papers to prevent her from serving another camp. This the first time that I mention it because I was always ashamed of the affair.

In addition to the counselors, senior counselors, and the doctor, there were the camper-waiters. Many wonderful boys served as camper-waiters, a job which in which they paid us for the privilege of exploiting them. Not only were they expected to set the tables and wait on the campers' tables, they were called upon for other duties: sorting the silverware, unloading trucks that brought supplies, preparing the cookouts, and so on. Each season was a tug-of-war as I tried to get labor out of them and they resisted in all ways possible. It was friendly war and rarely exploded into anger. When I found they worked harder when tips were involved, I worked out a system of rewards by assigning the best of them to work during guest weekends when they got tips.

As a group the camper-waiters were clever, happy and terribly funny—and the most messy campers ever. Their bunk was always a horror house and subject to closure by the Board of Health. My nephew Arnie and my wife's cousin Michael were just as messy as the worst of them. I can remember many of the waiters: Heshie Drazin, Mickey Turoff, Steven Berr, Charlie Barr. I tend to remember the first seasons much better, just as I still remember my first teaching class in Jerry's school in Bedford Stuyvesant much better than my later ones. The first of anything—kiss, lover, job—s always the most indelible and evokes the most nostalgia.

Both the camper-waiters and the counselors were participants in the many Indian rituals we had over the summer. I should say that most of these were totally fake Indian rituals. All camps during the period of the late 1940s and 1950s relied heavily on Indian lore. It was a carryover of the trend established by rich WASPs to send their children, usually boys only, to rugged, primitive outdoor camps so they would have some appreciation of indoor plumbing and central heating. Most of the early camps, and even later ones, had Indian or Indian-sounding names. There was a reliance on Indian dress, dances, campfires, songs and stories—especially songs and stories. The stories soon degenerated into ghost stories and tales designed to frighten the younger campers with some dreaded boy-eating creature of the deep dark woods.

I loved the songs. They were all new to me. I can recall "Gitchee Gummi" and our own Camp Brydon Lake song, among others. I was featured in the welcoming song, in the line: "We know you're hungry, eat your fill, Uncle Milton pays the bill." Even 40 years later these songs evoke a joy, a sadness, a nostalgia matched only by my recall of army songs and companions. In fact just last winter, Selma and I attended a birthday party and some six former campers were there. We all gathered around a piano and lustily sang all of the camp songs we could recall, laughing, crying and having helluva time.

In addition to campfires, Indians meant canoes, so we bought some. They were used in various ceremonies in addition to general use at the waterfront. At the end of one summer, we used two canoes, one paddled by some idiot counselors, to haul large numerals indicating the current year into the middle of the lake where the 'year' would be burnt, symbolizing the end of the camp season. Since the counselors thought the numbers might not burn properly, they doused them with gasoline, which dripped into the bottoms of the canoes. When the year was ignited, the canoes also burned. None of the crews were hurt. They swam ashore while the canoes burned as spectacularly as a Viking funeral.

Indian lore led me to one of my greatest and most amusing fiascos. I saw a canvas teepee for sale in a magazine and without consulting Jerry, I ordered one with the idea that it would serve as an adjunct to the campfire ceremonies as well as an Art and Crafts project involving painting Indian themes on the sides.

When it arrived, I was baffled. It was about 12 feet high and 16 feet in diameter and required some 12 poles to stand erect.

With the waiters' help I cut the poles and then we tried to erect it on the lower field near the lake. No matter how we struggled the dammed thing was always leaning one way or another.

Time after time the waiters reset the poles and each time the teepee was even more lop-sided. I grew angrier and angrier at each failure. It seemed impossible for such a simple project to be beyond a school principal.

I raged at them and at the inanimate object of my ire. Then Mickey Turoff, an extremely funny boy, said, "No wonder they called the Indians savages: they had to contend with this every day!"

I exploded into laughter and then we all walked away from the teepee. It stood there forlornly for days, until I asked some handymen to set it up for us. I often wonder what eventually happened to that heavy, awkward and hateful object.

Mr. Anderson and Tom the Chef

Mr. Anderson ran a neighboring farm. As a mark of respect, we never called him by his first name, Hendrick. Our first season he drifted up to see what the crazy New Yorkers were doing to a good dairy farm. He knew much more than we did and his suggestions about water pipes, foundations and sewer lines were always good ones, so we tended to look on him as a sort of mentor. He announced that since he was now 70—he looked much younger—and on Social Security, he could work for us during the summer and act as a caretaker during the winter. We hired him immediately and he was the best employee we ever had. He worked for us for 15 years and for our successors for at least five, so he was still active, and I mean sturdily active, until he was at least 90.

As we walked around the grounds together on our unending chores, Mr. Anderson would describe how the stone walls that marked off each field had been made and how snakes would sun themselves there. He talked about the great winter mapling times when the whole town assembled to tap the trees and boil the sap. He told of the happy shivarees, the custom of noisily visiting newlyweds on their first night together and surrounding them with gales of laughter. He would point out trees—hard maple, wild cherry, oak, fir, pine, beech—all valuable hardwoods and potentially valuable resources, as well as other flora, such as choke cherries (poisonous) and gooseberries (delicious). He was eager to share his knowledge and I was always interested in growing things. (I even had a flourishing "garden" on my windowsills in the Bronx until the Fire Department made me take it down for fear that the pots would fall into the street.) So I found these tours interesting and instructive. Every situation really is a learning situation if you take advantage of it.

I can still see Mr. Anderson in the hot sun, steadily and powerfully swinging a large scythe, cutting our lawns before we were bright enough or rich enough to buy a power mower. Farmers had to be versatile and he could do anything, from fixing a sewer line, to erecting a fence, operating machinery, putting out the waterfront floats and painting a bunk. He never took a day off. Sick or not, he came over. Even when he buried his wife, and several years later, a son, he came to work on the afternoon after the funerals.

Mrs. Anderson, a rail-thin woman, was a wonderful cook and a cheerful person who loved her flower garden. Jerry adored her blueberry pancakes with homemade maple syrup. As she was dying of cancer in the Delhi hospital, I visited her. She asked me not to look at her (she was terribly emaciated) because she wanted me to remember only how she looked before she was ill. I cried all of the way home and I never saw her alive again.

Mr. Anderson was given to pithy statements that I found hilarious. He would say about heavy loads, "As you start up the hill, it weighs like a lamb, but as you get to the top it turns into a full-sized sheep." Another comment was "Mountains are a good place to walk. If you get tired going up, just turn around and go down." My niece remembers hearing about a time when he volunteered to help clean the dishes.

Late in the evening, many hours after he had started, Helen came upon him still working and expressed amazement. He turned and said with great seriousness, "There are two sides to every dish."

His favorite drinks were milk and water from our spring. He never touched coke or beer, except for "yinya," that is, ginger beer. One night when we visited his home we got into a discussion about maple trees and what he called in his Norwegian accent "balling pins." Jerry and I kept asking what? what? We had no idea what he meant. The more we offered alternative meanings, the angrier he got, until he went to a back room and brought out a bowling pin cut from a maple log on our premises.

He never lost his temper, although we must have tried his patience with our stupidity. He had little in common with his neighbors, settlers of basic Anglo-Saxon Yankee stock, because he thought many of them were lazy and given to drink, especially the members of the Andes fire department, who held an annual picnic on the other side of the lake. He was a wonderful old but ever-young man.

Another camp character was Tom the Chef.

When Selma and I took over the kitchen, we were totally ignorant of what was involved in such a complex enterprise. We knew nothing of preparing meals for a large group or making large purchases in advance of the camp season (not that we had the money for that anyway) or how many people were actually required to operate a kitchen. We tried to cover any short fall of labor by extending our own time, strength and efforts to cover the situation. Like a tall man with a short blanket, every pull in one direction left us exposed in another.

Our first hirings were done by our short-lived third partner.

He hired an army buddy of his named Gus because he would work for low wages, and, as an army cook, he knew how to fire the gasoline army field kitchens without blowing us up. Gus brought with him his wife, Frieda, a pleasant, hard-working woman. But she had had recent surgery for breast cancer and couldn't work much, although she tried her best. Gus was also a very nervous type and the pounding from the boys playing basketball on the rec hall floor, which was the kitchen's ceiling, drove him mad. So he would go up to the recreation hall and slash all of the basketballs he could find, to Jerry's rage and horror. Caught in between, I tried to get the boys to play outdoors while meals were being prepared.

Gus and his wife worked for us for two years, but it was obvious that they lacked initiative and a flair for attractive meals, so we sought other help. We hired the chef of the Yale Faculty Club. He visited the camp and was aghast at the primitive fixtures and equipment and the large numbers he would have to feed, so he quit before he started. Hastily looking about because the season was about to start, we found a Lebanese Christian who had just quit working for the Boy Scouts Jamboree (in a huff) and Tom the Chef entered our lives.

Tom was an experienced, bright, hard working, reasonably honest and creative chef with a large burly frame, an incongruous mustache and a very terrible temper. He knew everything there was to do: ordering food, purchasing fresh vegetables at farmer's markets, hiring and training the kitchen girls, yelling at the waiters, baking and decorating cakes, and setting up marvelous end-of-the-season camp banquets and weekly smorgasbord buffets for the parents. He would also quit several times a season. I would also fire him several times a season. But we managed to lurch noisily through 13 seasons together without any homicide. One requirement: he refused to answer to any name or title except "chef."

He was a ferocious personality and Selma and I were the only people who were not afraid of him. In fact, he adored Selma and she could get him to do almost anything, like a gypsy child leading a surly dancing bear through its paces.

Tom taught me everything: how to keep the kitchen and dining room clean and attractive without buying any new stuff; how to buy inexpensive china and silverware; how to cook 300 pancakes an hour; how to keep the waiters working; how to exercise reasonable portion control on the meat items; how to allot ice cream and orange juice; how to bake and decorate the frequent sheet cakes, starting from scratch, no mixes allowed. Only in the area of butchering and meat cutting did he admit my superiority. However, when we went deer hunting together out of season, I was amazed at his skill in gutting and skinning our trophy deer.

He would come up to camp two weeks early and visit all of the local farms seeking out big, strong and willing girls to train as salad girls and cook's assistants. He was good at selecting them and we never had a dud—stupid, yes, but always willing.

As I look back, I think a large amount of his fierceness was related to his many ailments, including having almost every bone broken and all of his teeth knocked out in a terrible auto accident and a continuing battle with diabetes. Much of it was for show to protect his opinion of his status and his need for respect. But he really liked all of us. In fact, for more than 35 years after he worked for us, we still visited him on our trips down to Florida. At the age of 86, he has Alzheimers and I am not certain who he thinks we are.

He refused to work for our successors and I got him a job

with another camp owner. He worked there for several years, with each side constantly complaining to me. Finally both sides were thoroughly sick of the other and he quit to go to work for a large industrial feeding company.

He married three times and I knew all of his wives. That alone would make an interesting story someday. I thought of him as not particularly good-looking, but all of his wives were attractive. He must have had some assets in that area that eluded me.

The History of Brydon and the Lake

I have inserted this section in response to my niece's query about the name "Brydon Lake." It has an interesting history. To set the stage, I should start with a piece of Catskill history. While most of the land around the camp was being developed by towns like Ithaca, Syracuse, Delhi and Walton, our area was left largely undeveloped for two centuries because of the famous Hardenburgh Patent. This was a grant from the Netherlands Crown to a Herr Hardenburgh, who had the right and the obligation to take this uninhabited land and fill it with industrious farmers and so provide goods and taxes for the king.

Unfortunately, the Hardenburghs, a hard-headed stubborn people, got into a terrible conflict over how the land would be divided up among the family. Each attempt at a legal or a negotiated settlement failed and the generations went by until there were now hundreds of claimants for the land. No one could buy or sell any of the land, because no one could assure the purchaser of a clear title. Some lawyers spent their entire careers in that vortex of angry claims and counterclaim. So a large part of the land, except for minor bits of farming and logging, was permitted to lie idle. Eventually the courts, thoroughly sick of the angry mess, ruled that whoever held the land now and had paid taxes on it for a certain period was the rightful owner and all other claims were void. Now people could sell the land with a clear title—and, many years later, our brave pioneers from Far Rockaway were among the purchasers.

The land was poor, but in addition to being used for some farming, it produced hides and tannin from the tree bark. So a large leather industry flourished, supplying the newly industrial towns with leather goods: gloves, straps, machinery belts, luggage, and most of all harnesses and saddles. Hence the growing towns of Tannersville and Gloversville nearby.

Incidentally, the name Catskill has nothing to do with "cats." It is a corruption of the Dutch word Katters Kill, used by the initial Dutch Patroon settlers, which meant a crooked or diagonal stream or small river. The same root is used in the term "Katter Corner" for diagonal locations. (If that it not true, it is probably a better story than the real one.)

Going back to the history of the camp, the campground, about 500 acres, including the lake, had originally been a land grant given to a Captain Adam Bryden (note the spelling) for his service in the Revolutionary War. The state had no money for mustering-out pay so they gave out free land to "deserving" veterans. Most sold their land and pocketed the money. Capt. Bryden was made of sterner stuff. He built a house, barn and several sheds and became a dairy farmer. The soil was too poor to grow anything but grass, which the milk-making machines called cows turned into salable milk and other dairy products.

He had two daughters; one married a Mr. Sutherland and the other married another farmer whose name is lost in my memory. As was customary, when Adam died he left his farm to both daughters to be shared equally. The two brothers-in-law could not get along, so they divided the farm and the lake reasonably equally and the Sutherlands lived on the side that we initially purchased.

The two brothers-in-law were constantly at war with each other and I found records in the country seat of the two families going to court some forty times in the previous century! What was the feud about? Everything and nothing: one was cutting too much ice from his share of the lake; one was letting his cows or pigs roam loose and damage the other's vegetable garden; one let his fences fall into disrepair; one cut too much timber or let the lake fall too low or made too much noise or just simply existed.

For spite, the other family sold out to a disreputable family and the Sutherlands were left alone with awful neighbors, until the two original camp partners from Rockaway arrived to buy them out for the magnificent sum of $12,000.

One partner, a man with no taste and less sense, thought the name Brydon with an "o" was classier than the "e" version (despite the fact that the lake was spelled with an "e" on county maps) and that was stuck on the camp. (Later I even made a play on words by naming the camp newspaper, the Brydon Groom. What brilliance!)

The property had a small cemetery with seven graves, high on the hill, for the Sutherland family. Prior to the advent of communal cemeteries, it was customary to bury your dead on your own land. When I discovered it, I had the workers bulldoze a high earthen wall around it so that campers would not inadvertently walk on this ground. I think the earthen wall is still there and the dead lie undisturbed, although the headstones, surely illegible by now, may have fallen over.

One afternoon I saw three very elderly white-haired ladies come onto our grounds. They introduced themselves as the Sutherland girls—"girls" because they were still "maiden ladies." They apologetically asked if they could see the "Old Homestead."

I was delighted by the visit and we toured the whole camp. They kept exclaiming over everything. "This is where the blacksmith shed was." "This was where we stored the hay and silage." "This was where the cows were milked." They even mentioned the names of some of the bovines. They marveled at all of the "wonders" we had installed on their "Home Place." When they left, after graciously thanking me, the names on the tombstones suddenly had meaning. I felt that I had touched history and been touched by it and now had a respectful insight into how people lived 100 years before the camp was built. I regret that I never saw any of those charming women again.

Historically, one of the major moneymakers of the old farm was the lake, and it was always a special place for me.

The lake was a great renewable asset because every winter the owners would saw enormous blocks of ice out of its frozen surface, cover them with a blanket of sawdust and sledge them down to the nearest railroad line (probably Arkville, next to Margarettville) and ship them to the vast ice houses in Manhattan or Brooklyn. It was the only source of cooling for food or drinks until mechanical refrigeration was invented. Catskill ice commanded a high price because it was the finest: blue-white, dense and sparkling crystalline and highly desired.

The ice eventually brought men seeking water for the thirsty metropolis. They built large dams across the valleys and ended up drowning two towns, Pepacton and Downsville, to create reservoirs that provided the city with water. I wrote an account called "The Drowned Towns" that described the legal battles and emotional costs of having one's land taken by eminent domain to provide comfort to strangers.

When we were deciding whether or not to invest in the camp, both Jerry and I felt that the most wonderful feature of the land was the 30-acre spring-fed lake in the middle of the property. It caught our eye initially and was what "made" the camp.

Unfortunately, we were too stupid to note that 4/5 of the lake lay on the property on the other side of the lake from the campgrounds, and that the dam that set the height of the water in the lake was on that other side. By lifting the gate of their dam, the owners of that property could make the waterfront on our side disappear and we would be left with a muddy rim as our "waterfront." We had just learned an expensive lesson in riparian (water) rights.

We were over a barrel, so I went next door to negotiate with the awful people who lived there, descendents of the disreputable neighbors who had lived next-door to the Sutherlands. They were the most detested family in the county, whose origin went back to British and Hessian soldiers who had deserted during the Revolution and married with runaway slaves and Indians as well as debtors and criminals. Their house was an incredible slatternly building. Even Gypsies were more orderly than they. They also neglected to send their children to school and lived by strategic stealing from their neighbors, illegal logging, hunting and fishing, plus a bit of day labor and welfare.

My visit to them was like a visit to Tobacco Road. The matron of the tribe, a heavy woman chewing on a straw, with several dirty raggedy children clinging to her dirty skirts, was the chief negotiator. Helen accompanied me and she and I played it cool and made a neighborly proposition. Since we had no need for the fodder from our fields, we would permit them to cut our hay before and after the camp season free. We would have neatly cut fields and they would have free fodder for the whole winter for their few cows. However, steady labor was not their style and the fields were often left uncut. In addition, they became a nuisance coming over to our land with their cows. (Once the cows invaded when Helen was left alone in the main house. Even from the lake, where we were swimming, we could hear her plaintive shrieks of "Shoo, cow, shoo!")

So we went back and I offered them a few hundred dollars to fix their fences and keep their cows at home. I never mentioned the lake or its potential value to them. Eventually, they were taught by another neighbor that they had a valuable asset, so they asked for the astronomical sum of $1,000 for the annual rent, never expecting to get it. They happily settled for $400. I knew we were in grave danger, so we decided to make them an offer they could not refuse. Pretending that I was not really interested in the land, I made a token offer of $5,000 and they seemed eager to sell. It was more money than they had seen in a generation. But they haggled. Worried that they would get real advice, I settled for $5,000 down and a twenty-year mortgage paying some $1,000 every year. They sold and we bought, adding 220 acres to our original 220 and gaining peace of mind as well as two buildings, one for the future infirmary when we finally got it cleaned out and a falling-down horse barn for our riding groups.

The lake needed a built-up waterfront for safe swimming and a place to change. So we did what we always did: built on the cheap. Instead of investing in a commercially developed and constructed waterfront fixture, we bought old oil drums and somehow fastened these unwieldy and dangerous things to homemade walks and placed them out into the lake. They were very unsteady, no matter how we tried to anchor them. One got seasick just by walking on them.

I can remember cousin Monroe helping to put out the walks so proudly made by Jerry. They tipped over, hurling Monroe into the lake and all of his precious cigars floated away, to his fury. After several years of that rickety arrangement, we finally bought the needed walks and floats and built a proud deck for changing clothing.

The lake was the happy focus of many camp activities. Twice a day children would assemble for swimming and instruction. The older boys challenged their manhood by swimming across the lake, about 3/4 of a mile, accompanied by a counselor in a rowboat. (My niece reminds me that girls also took up this challenge. She succeeded in swimming across the lake and back, motivated by the swimming counselor's promise, unfulfilled, of chocolate-covered cherries. My daughter also swam the lake.) Those who could make a round trip were honored in the camp ceremonies and in the newsletter. The lake was completely off limits at night or when no counselor was present. We were terrified at the thought of a drowning. One occurred in some camp every season.

Fishing for sunfish and other lake fish was very popular, as was canoeing. We had purchased good and expensive canoes because even Jerry was not prepared to make an aluminum canoe that floated right side up. Once we bought an old wooden fishing skiff. It was so heavy that four men could get a hernia taking it down to the lake and even worse taking it back. It always leaked and no one, not even Mr. Anderson, could ever find out why. I eventually consigned it to a special Indian ceremony and watched with delight when it was burned.

At dusk we would have lakeside sings, story telling, and Indian dances (made up in Brooklyn). We often assembled to watch the sun dip into the lake or attend a canoe fire ceremony.

One particularly beautiful ceremony took place the night after the end of Color War, when, as I described earlier, the numbers of the year just past, such as "1954," were burned in a canoe and then a second canoe would reveal the next year in flames, to loud applause, songs and tears. On the last night of the season, campers would light small candles attached to little squares of wood, make a wish, and set them on the lake, to drift out as a throng of twinkling lights. It was all shmaltzy but quite moving and impressive.

When I had a rare free moment, I would take out a small sunfish sailboat and drift quietly on the lake, unwinding. But best of all I loved the lake early in the morning, when I rose to go to the kitchen. With the sun coming up and the lake eerily shrouded in a cloak of mist, it looked like something magical out *The Lady and the Lake.* I was greeted by woodchucks popping up to see who the intruder was and hundreds of chirping goldfinches that perched on our telephone wires. It was a rare place—a place dreams were made of. I hated and loved that place with the same strong passionate ambivalent feelings.

All Through the Year

My first year at the camp I ignorantly assumed that camp business would be a two-month affair. Little did I know of the endless preparation and detailed work required prior to and after the summer. All through the year one spent endless days and nights hiring staff, planning menus and activities, purchasing food for June delivery, soliciting for campers, writing a camp newsletter and organizing the camp reunion. It was basically having a second job in addition to our teaching jobs.

Jerry planned activities and did most of the work of getting campers. His wife Helen remembered standing in the hall of their first apartment building with a roll of nickels, using the pay phone to set up appointments with the families of prospective campers. Selma was in charge of planning menus and purchasing food, with help from Mr. Anderson. I assisted with hiring and took on the responsibility of the newsletter.

The entire enterprise of the newsletter was a most amateurish affair. None of us knew anything about simple things like how to mimeograph, where to get artwork, or the simple mechanics of editing and doing effective layouts. Today, after several decades of working on and being editor-in-chief of my temple's prize-winning literary magazine, *The Light,* I could be expected to turn out a respectable publication.

But at the time it was horrible. I cringe as I think back at the quality—or lack of quality—of that terrible newsletter. It was carefully mistyped and stapled together and we had the chutzpah to send it out as sales device for the next season. What idiots we were! I wonder why anyone would take us seriously when this representative of the camp came in the mail.

I can only think that the parents were forgiving and thought that this crude offering was consistent with our "primitive" camp ambiance and facilities—or they simply went through the publication to find the names of their children and gloat over their various honors and achievements. In later years, I made certain that we constantly listed the names of campers, as often as possible in every issue. (I think we had two or three issues every winter.) It was a significant part of our recruitment campaign and we should have had professional help or at least a printer to do the newsletter. But as usual, we did it at no cost and I suspect we may have lost campers because of this frugality. It certainly did not help the camp image, even though we were childishly proud of our efforts.

I don't recall who wrote and typed the earliest issue—I suspect Helen and Selma as typists did the work on the small manual typewriter. All of the issues had frequent typos, especially when the burden of producing the magazine fell on me, a world-class klutz when it came to typing. I know that I must be wrong, but I have the distinct impression that I was the main worker on *The Brydon Groom*. Perhaps it was because as an assistant principal, I had access to the school's mimeograph machine. I would stay in school late to run off the latest issue. My niece remembers her whole family sitting in front of the television in the evening, collating and stapling together issues of the newsletter.

When we discovered rexographs, we added color, at least to the covers, and I was the artist who drew or copied the artwork. It wasn't bad—it was awful. The publication grew from two sheets to a six or eight sheet magnum opus and we began eventually to have articles, usually in praise of a camper, riddles, puzzles and other sundry attractions for the children.

As I recall we had great difficulty getting grist for our mill. Despite our pleas, the campers did not send us any material about their activities in school or at home so we had to call and find out "what's doing" to get items for the newsletter.

I used to have a full set of all of the issues we printed, but years ago in a fit of cleanliness, Selma and I tossed them out. It would have been nice to look through one or more of the issues, even if only to laugh at it.

Another major effort during the year was the camp reunion. Initially I knew nothing about camp reunions, so I had to rely on Jerry for guidance in this area. I think we did not have one after the first season, but I may be wrong.

One of the earlier reunions took place in a summer day camp or beach resort somewhere in Far Rockaway. It was crowded and dingy and we ran out of food, even though we only served franks and hamburgers. It was a public relations disaster.

Later years we had the affair at the George Washington Hotel on Fifth Avenue, a far more reputable and attractive place. I am not sure the reunions were successful in seducing the campers to return the next year. Just as many non-signers for the next season showed up as did those who were willing to return. Most were just coming to meet their summer friends. I think we made a strategic error in never inviting some of the more popular counselors to appear, even if we had to pay their travel expenses to the event. We were too frugal, or too unthinking, for our own good.

With all of this work during the year and all the responsibilities during the summer, we were too busy and tense to notice how our own children fared as campers. They knew that as the directors' children, they were required to follow all the rules and set a good example for other campers. But it wasn't until many years after the camp had been sold that I wondered what their camp experiences were like.

Now I know from talking to my daughter Emily, my nephew Arnie and my niece Joanne that the camp made a much greater impression on them than any of us adults realized at the time. For them, summers spent at Brydon Lake seemed like a natural and unchanging part of life, since they had always gone there. They especially enjoyed the weeks at the beginning and end of the summer when there were no campers present. Then they roamed the sprawling grounds as they wished, collecting wild strawberries, fishing in the lake, and exploring the wilderness. They could rummage at will through the costume room, used when the campers put on shows. They even put on little performances on the huge rec hall stage to a small audience of their parents and the few other staff members who arrived early. As the children grew older, we also gave them responsibilities. Before the season opened, they would trudge to each bunk distributing brooms and wastebaskets. After the season ended, they were allowed to keep the spoils that campers had left behind, such as comic books and candy. They would also harvest the vegetables sown as part of the gardening activity, and we would all enjoy the fruits of the campers' labors.

Emily has told me that she enjoyed camp so much that it was one of the highlights of her life. I was too busy to really observe her, but some anecdotes stand out. Once when she was about four, she appeared before the small shack that served as our canteen. She had her cousin Arnie, a sweet and obliging child, about the same age, in tow. It was obvious who was the leader of this expedition. She loudly demanded that she be given some "salivas." The counselor in charge was puzzled and showed her his other wares, gum, books, chocolate. She continued to shout and stamp her foot that she wanted nothing but "salivas." Through all this, Arnie stood by quietly. Since she was the owner's daughter and not really a camper at that age, the counselors were fearful of offending me, so I was called to find out what she really wanted. I showed her other items and finally was successful when I showed her a roll of Lifesavers. "That's it, salivas!" she cried, snatched the item from my hand and escorted Arnie off the scene to share the loot.

From the time she could talk, Emily wanted to leave the directors' cottage and go up to the bunks. Though that would have helped us, she was too young. Finally the year she was five, she wheedled me into letting her sleep in the freshman bunk. She pulled her small suitcase, laden with clothing and other sundry items, up to the bunk, while I watched with amusement. About an hour later, she came down from the bunk, hauling her suitcase behind her. "Oh no!" I exclaimed. "You wanted to go, now you have to adjust and you must stay there."

I was nonplused when she cried, "I only came down for my comic books."

Once we had some income we would spend a few days after the camp season at Kass' Inn to unwind and recover from the rigors of the season. One morning I came down for breakfast and found Emily (about five) and Arnie eating huge sundaes. I asked Emily what this meant. "Oh," she said, "they will give you anything if you just say 'charge it!'"

All of our children say they have wonderful memories of the camp. Spending every summer together was a major factor in creating a close bond between the cousins, one that lasts today. They tell me that they love looking at old camp photographs and memorabilia, singing the camp songs, and reminiscing about their various adventures. I can see now that while Helen, Jerry, Selma and I were busy running the camp, we were also storing up wonderful memories as well. In later years we could still recall many former campers and counselors, as well as our myriad disasters and successes. Looking back, I see the hard work and struggle required to make the camp a success, but I also see all the camaraderie and joy and fun we shared. I get great pleasure from reminiscing about camp days, but what I said of the lake I can say of the camp as a whole: I hated and loved that place with the same strong passionate ambivalent feelings.

The Parable of the Drowned Town

The city needed water, so the town had to die.

The great colossus of the city needed a reservoir so that it could assuage its thirsty millions through its vast network of aqueducts and water treatment plants.

The city was first attracted to the valley by the ice, the cold clear ice that had been sawn out of the blue lakes and sledged to the city where it lay in great sawdust covered icehouses. Delicious ice—Catskills ice—it was advertised as the best. It was a great resource, regenerating and non-polluting. As soon as some was cut by men sweating in the bitter cold, it was replaced by the hoary breath of winter.

This was a cruel land despite its beauty. It had very limited resources. There were trees and there was sandstone and there were animals. The local people sold the sandstone to the city, where it was used to build endless rows of middle class homes that stood staring at each other. The animal pelts were sold to the great leather tanners, the glovers and belt makers. In a society dependent on the horse, there was a limitless demand for leather goods: baggage harnesses, saddles and the massive belts that turned the early factory machines. Elegant ladies and horses wore the products produced by the small but thriving towns to the north.

So the area furnished the sandstone and the fir trees and the hides that served important industries until the trees ran out and the topsoil flowed downstream.

The hardscrabble farms with soil too thin for most crops could produce little but grass. So the farmers grew milk, as they did in Switzerland. The great milk-making machines called cows would convert the succulent grasses into rivers of white, creamy milk.

It was a hard disciplined life. Cows needed attention twice a day, every day of the year, even on church days. The dairymen did not even have the slack time of winter that crop farmers had. One needed to fight one's way to the barn through the deep snow and the fury of winter's blasts, because cows needed feeding and milking.

There were breaks in the monotony: weddings, graduations, parades and funerals. During the great winter mapling times, the whole community gathered together in a great sap boiling enterprise. Miles of maple trees were tapped and the great boilers would reduce the thin sap to thick, incredibly sweet syrup. A sample ladle of the hot maple syrup would be flung on the virgin snow and the children would scramble for the icy yet hot, tasty confection that formed.

Now the city was reaching out to grasp them and the city men came north, looked into the pleasant valleys and found a site inhabited by a small lovely hamlet. It was not a great town and produced no one of renown. The inhabitants were a hardy people. They had lived there in the tall mountains, with their bitter frosts and rolling thunders of summer storms, for more than 200 years. Most were of English descent with a slight admixture of Dutch, German, and Scandinavian, with names like Hoag, Harvey, Woolheater and Anderson. The same names were repeated for centuries on the tax rolls and the cemetery stones. On the wall of the public library was the roster of the Civil War regiment that had marched forth from the town and on it were the same names that one still met on the town streets.

Now the city people told them they would have to leave. They said that the city needed the valley and the river. After they built a dam, the river would flood the valley and there would be no room for the town.

The people wanted to resist, but the city had the right under the state's power of eminent domain to confiscate any needed lands, for a price. So while they thought of resorting to arms, cooler heads prevailed. They fell back on the last resource of the citizenry in a democracy: they banded together and hired lawyers.

What is a fair price for a farm? What is fair for a small country store, a town lot, an acre of woodland? What is the worth of a house in which several generations of one family have lived, loved and suffered? Each item became a matter of bitter dispute. The farmers set what they thought were fair prices and the city appraisers offered far less.

But who could really blame the two sides for not coming to an understanding? They were buying and selling different things. The city was buying acreage, a farm, a plot, a building, a barn or a fence post.

The farmers were selling something totally different. They were selling a garden patch painfully torn from the stone-encrusted ground by a beloved grandmother. They were selling a barn whose weather-beaten sides still carried the sweat of the fathers, brothers and uncles who had raised it. They were selling miles of stone fences whose stones had been painfully dragged, over the generations, from the niggardly fields. They were selling memories of cooperative barn-raisings and enormous picnics.

How could they price the small cottage where the whole town had gathered for a great shivaree to gleefully welcome newlyweds to their new marital beds?

How could you sell the ground still stained by the blood of an uncle who was gored there by a bull? They were being asked to sell the sweet blackberries bushes they had picked and the noble apple trees whose branches they had climbed as children.

The city people were just buying land while the residents were selling lives and the memories that made up those lives. So they could never come together on a just price, especially since the farmers and townsfolk really did not want to sell at any price.

The claims and counterclaims went on for many years as the town fought what amounted to the confiscation of a large valley to benefit strangers. But finally the city won the last court battle and the people were informed that they had to move. Some still threatened to defend their land with their shotguns, just as they had fought off Redcoat and Indian attacks. The courts and the bulldozers and the sheriff's battalions convinced them that it would be fruitless.

So the farms were emptied and the cattle and equipment were sold off. Buildings were auctioned to anyone who offered to move them, and many were sold. One could buy a large farmhouse that had housed a whole family for six hundred dollars, with the one proviso that one had to lift and cart it away to a new location within a short period of time. Some buildings were obviously not moveable, particularly the better ones made of brick or stone. So a small woodshed ended up being worth more than the town's steepled church.

One thing the town and country folk refused to do was to

leave their dead behind. The city agreed; the cemeteries, even the small private ones, would be emptied. The city would pay the expenses of burial anywhere else in the county.

Young, strong farmers came, attracted by the offer of work digging up the old graves. Within the newer graves, those only thirty or forty years old, the remnants of the coffin often contained something; bones, false teeth, glasses. Even a bit of jewelry at times, a ring, a locket, buried with a beloved one. The really old graves usually produced nothing, except that as one dug deep, one became more aware that this was a grave. The ground appeared deeper in color, browner, as traces of the coffin and traces of the coffined were found enriching the soil.

The headstones were frequently illegible. The soft sandstone markers, so favored in early times because they were easier to carve, were also softer for the elements to erase.

Each grave was carefully marked, and carefully dug up and respectfully transported elsewhere. Finally all of the graves were emptied, the church and the farms were emptied, and the town lay there quiet, open, sad and uninhabited

Engineers and monstrous machines erected the great dam across the small river. When the dam was completed, the water began to rise and covered the fields and the fences. The word spread among the farmers and townsfolk.

They and their children came. They stood on the high hills looking down into the valley and watched the waters rising. They saw the dusty streets that they had run on as children being covered up. The many ponds on which they had skated in the frozen winters merged into the miles-long lake that was forming. The trees, the berry bushes, the trysting places—all covered over.

Then the waters lapped at the structures and the sheds and

the small homes and the little farms were gone. And then the larger houses, clapboarded, steep-sided and many-gabled, were covered.

Finally only the church bell tower still projected above the rising waters like a hand pleading to God. The bell in the steeple slowly and softly bonged, bonged, bonged, as it tolled the death of the hamlet. The waters quietly, slowly, but inexorably rose until they covered over church steeple and silenced the bell.

The people gazed down in silence as they stood there for weeks, watching their town disappear. Finally the waters were ten, twenty, forty feet deep over the church steeple. Deeper, deeper into the cold dark waters the town lay as the reservoir rose and spread. The town remained below, a submarine entity. Fish swam through the windows and the rooms.

The townspeople and the farmers turned and looked at their children in silence. Without an outcry, without any weeping or wailing, they got into their wagons and left. None looked back. There was no need to. The town had been indelibly engraved in their memories. The vision of their town was printed in their brains and deeply carved into their hearts. While they lived, the town would live.

Deep in the dark cold waters, slowly and quietly, the bell swayed and tolled, mourning the lost and scattered people. The great thirsty city was indifferent to the plaintive tolling of the drowned town.

The town had died. Its only crime was that it stood in the way of the waters, the blessed living waters that were needed by the city to flourish. The flowing waters nourished the city and killed the town.

Family

Photo Gallery

To the distress of my wife, I collect pictures—albums of family and scenic photographs. The reason for my unreasonable passion in this matter is that my own memory is but a gallery of rapidly fading images. These other graphic representations are unchanging, eternally registering the radiant energy of the light that originally painted them on the silvered negatives. I can leisurely examine these fixed images time after time.

Like many people, I have hundreds of travel photographs that were taken on our many trips: me in front of the Eiffel Tower; my wife in front of the Western Wall; me gazing up at Abu Simbel; she gazing down from a balcony on Nantucket; both of us in front of a glacier or on top of a volcano; shopping in a souk or an Indian bazaar; getting on a plane or off a ship; leaning against the Sphinx; climbing the Spanish Steps or a path to the Acropolis or up a pyramid or the Great Divide.

It is all endless summers, trite poses, people gazing directly into the camera to shout "I've been here" and "Look at me."

We pose in front of a sign like "Selma, Alabama" or behind a sign like "Milton, Mass" or besides a sign like "Stier" in Bavaria because they are names, our IDs—curious and interesting only to us.

We pose near rocks; on rocks; on rocks; behind rocks; in front of, behind and even up a tree; once even through a tree in Yellowstone. All of this furor and effort because life is an adventure which will vanish. It is not true or permanent unless captured by the lens. Thus we betray our fear of being lost without a trace.

That is why I have always enjoyed looking at old photographs, edges cracked, corners missing and bent, faded to sepia. They are peaceful and sometimes pride-filled images of people and places long changed. They are haunting memories of people and places I never knew or experienced.

Each picture is a moment in time, caught like a remembered dream of languid youth, white-clad against a blue sky, caressed by a breeze that caresses forever, a day that will never cease, a tomorrow that will never come. No past, no future, just an endless now, caught in amber for eternity and remembered with fondness tinged with regret.

These old photos always fill me with nostalgia because whoever or whatever is portrayed in these silvered images, these slivers of preserved time, is gone, changed by the pressures of the calendar. As Shakespeare wrote, "Golden lads and girls all must, as chimney-sweepers, come to dust."

I recall a picture of a boy I never knew, a Civil War recruit, about 17 years old, proudly posing in his over-sized uniform, eyes sparkling, narrow chest inflated, innocence and excitement radiating from his face. I wonder to whom he sent this image. And I think of his bones moldering at Shiloh where he fell, moldering more than a half century before my birth, and I am sad, sad because I know what is going to happen to him. I look at him and I know his future, his all too short future, while he does not. His face is full of joy and he doesn't know what the next moment will bring.

He knows he will live forever. And he does. In my album he lives on—young, unchanging, happy and eager to be a soldier on the old campgrounds. The Minie ball and the grave have not yet touched him.

My examination of old family pictures is filled with poignancy. While the photo represents the present of a distant past, I know the future of those who paused before the lens. I know that the elfin boy portrayed mischievously, a bundle of energy, is now an elephantine man ponderously seeking a painless diet. The shy slender girl looking back coyly over one shoulder went from one troubled and unfortunate marriage and career choice to another, and is now no more, by her own choice. The manly scout in his Betar uniform is unaware that he will disappear into the maw of the camps and chimneys without a trace.

There is no hint of the future in these photographs. I look at these changeless moments and I am filled with anxiety and sorrow. Helpless, I try to shout words of advice and warning to these heedless relatives. That is the horror—to know and to be unable to change things.

Then there are the special photos. Among my favorite personal pictorial images is a photo of my two children splashing in the surf. Technically it is not particularly good as it is slightly blurred by the spray and out of focus, but it shows a wonderful moment of uninhibited pleasure, sheer animal spirits mingled with the obvious affection the children have for each other, truly brother and sister. I know that I am a fortunate father.

Another photo that never fails to touch me whenever I look at it is of my son when he was about ten years old. He is seated in the front of a canoe just as we started a trip down a white-water river. His uncertain smile is full of pride that I have given him the responsibility of paddling point, yet also shows he is immensely grateful that my strength and experience are there to support him in the coming crises. There is love, joy and respect in this image. What more can a parent ask of his child? It is more reward than one deserves.

I carefully scan a picture of my parents, an *Errinerungs Karte,* a postcard-sized photo designed to be distributed among family and friends. My father, gloved, wearing a stylish Homburg and a fur-collared Chesterfield coat, holds the arm of my mother, who is clad in the latest mode, a traveling suit. It marks the day that they left Czernovitz to come to America. Eyes front, gazing directly and confidently into the camera, they faced a long and dangerous journey into a strange land with courage and pride in their own strength and abilities, knowing that they may never return. That is why this photo was being taken. I realize that many copies were distributed to their many siblings, relatives and friends so that they would not be forgotten. And I realize that all of the copies, except for this sole survivor, were consumed in the Holocaust.

I am filled with pride as I look at it. They made a most handsome couple. In a harsh new environment they made a livelihood and raised a successful, well-educated brood. But as I look at their strong youthful faces, I see super-imposed their faces fifty years later. I know things that the photo delineations do not know, how things turned out for them and how things eventually ended for them, and I am filled with poignant grief.

My father was a strong man, a former army officer who exerted his influence through personality and physical strength. He never achieved his full potential. His uncompromising pride and sense of integrity and his language disadvantage held him back. My mother, while a marvelous homemaker and cook, bereft of the support of parents and siblings, became a bundle of fears and alarms that did not cease until she did.

I look at a photo taken by a street photographer showing me perched on a pony, as I would look at a photo of a stranger. The figure pictured is a stranger to me. It is not me and perhaps it never was. The arrogant posture; the over-wise eyes squinting into the sun, these have no relation to me or what I have become. It is a moment cast into eternal immobility that has no relevance or meaning to me.

While more recent pictures are more free in movement and posture because the cameras do not require the long rigid poses of early pictures, I still love the old breath-holding images. They project a strong sense of identity. "This is me! This is the way I choose to show myself to the world and to posterity!" There is a pride of place and position and possession in these old photographs. Uniforms, jewels and costumes are worn with pride and zest. This is my house. This is my wife, my family, my cow. All that is owned is eagerly displayed for the viewer's envy and appreciation. They say, "Gaze upon me, you beholder, and eat your heart out."

Sometimes when photos are viewed in time sequence they offer us clues that we ignored or which we did not perceive. Now we realize that the somber and unhappy faces shown by a beloved uncle were signaling a grave life-threatening illness. Pictures show some of the family always on the extreme periphery in the group shots. In retrospect, one realizes that this was an indication of later acts of alienation and withdrawal from the family.

Who is clutching whom? Who is always making silly faces and clowning? Grimacing? Looking off into the distance? Posing with hand on hip? As one looks at these pictures, over the years, with the benefit of hindsight, a pattern develops and a message emerges—one that the lens caught but the eye was too bemused to see at the time.

So many of my favorite images speak of unspoken love. My daughter, on her wedding day, smiling admiringly at her regal grandmother; my son tugging at my pants leg while he looks up with trust; cousins, different yet curiously alike, arms draped about each other and laughing at a family joke; young parents, bursting with pride, displaying their unremarkable progeny; friends waving bon voyage. All of these are parts of my dreams, my life and my memories—and I am grateful for all of them. Sometimes one encounters a family group shot and feels shock when one realizes that almost everyone depicted is dead. A glance at the date on the reverse side—so long ago! Such a short time ago! Again one looks at the faces, the postures for clues. Did they have any inkling? Was there any signal or aura being emitted? Life, I am grateful, conceals its ends so that we can be blissfully unaware of what our future holds.

What do all of these images, now often in living color, say or mean? In some they evoke a polite yawn or queries like, "What year was that?" or "What was the name of the dog?" Yet, as I wander through the meadows of my past, my albums, I sometimes begin to substitute the image for the reality, the image for the living, the past-future commingling with the future-past.

The preserved image, the delineation of the human face and form, has fascinated humanity since the cave days, and I carry on the tradition. The camera retains and recalls the sunny hours, the beach party, the vacation trip, the graduation. The personal camera doesn't visit the hospital ward or make shiva calls. It doesn't sit up with you in your bathrobe drinking tea while a child grows purple with the croup nor does it preserve the agony of an arthritic hip. It seizes and freezes the happy times, the best dressed occasions, the laughing toasts and the festive tables.

To others this collection of pictures is of little or no interest. It is an inert assemblage of wholly ordinary people and places. However, to me these images have a symbiotic relationship with me. The pictures stimulate and clarify my memories and my memories illuminate and animate the photos. As I look at them, they become active dioramas, full of sound, color, warmth and laughter. I hear the voices, smell the food, sense the breezes and feel the pressure of a loving embrace. I relive the scene and give life to it, as though the photos and I nourish each other.

These photos are not part of a dead museum. Under my eye they become filled with throngs of happy, noisy people and smiling faces, looking into a glorious untainted and undamaged future.

Momma's Tablecloth

Tisch-tuch[1]—teller of tales
Traces of simchas[2],
Marks of mournful family conferences,
Gravy stains left by the many now in the peace of the grave.
Here a mark of Elijah's cup,
Tracks of gatherings and partings.

Warp and woof born in a quiet shtetl[3],
Embroidered in the chatter of women.
Pristine greeter of the Sabbath Queen,
Frail as the smoke of the Havdalah[4] candles

A spread with wine, bread and peace
Contrast the gleaming silver and crystal
A background that holds the foreground—conflict and contentment

Edges frayed, the slight tear
The rose-knots faded like the cheek of the girl who created this—
Nahden[5] for the man she had not yet met.

Fluttering cloud poised over the table
Settling with a soft sigh,
Supple folds gracefully descending, "Ah zoy kikt ohs a tisch.[6]"

Web of dreams and drama
Center of delights and trauma
Witness to all—marking the times of joining and unjoining.

Yellowed folds shaped by the drawer,
China closet as draper/fuller
Prayers, laughs, shouts and jokes etched the air over it.

Source of pride and vanity
Guarded by the stiff red velvet sentinel chairs
Sign that all is transient but love

Cream-colored reminder of sojourners
Who have journeyed on, yet are recalled,
Stains silently tracing events
Frail yet strong with love remembered.
Silent eloquent uniter of family
Centerpiece of family images,
Tisch-tuch—teller of elapsed time.

¹Tablecloth
²Joys
³Jewish ghetto
⁴End of the Sabbath
⁵Dowery
⁶That's what a tablecloth should look like.

To a Daughter on the Approach of Her 40th Birthday

When one is young, the summers and the years stretch forth as golden eternities. There is so much time and it seems to move so slowly. Growing up takes forever. Yet while the days may pass slowly, the years fly. Suddenly one is an adult who has accumulated a whole packet of years.

The approach of one's fortieth birthday was always viewed with great trepidation because it presaged the imminent onset of senescence. Today, with improved drugs, medical technology and greater awareness of diet and exercise, this is no longer so feared an event. But reaching forty is still a most significant occasion. One has reached a plateau and the zenith, the meridian, of one's life is past. From now on, many of the shadows will be in front of you, coloring and adding depth and perspective to your view of life.

One's fortieth birthday is a time for reflection and a review of the major decisions and achievements of your life. By now you realize that many earlier options and choices are closed to you, that you will not be able to do some of the things you dreamed of as a young adult.

That is not all bad. Dangerous shoals and impossible choices have been avoided. Career decisions that have worked are now part of your history and memories. Wonderful, bright and healthy children and a loving and respecting husband are things to cherish and enjoy. You, I am blessed to report, have really done it all—marriage, children, career.

Work, honors, grants, books, are all on the record and one now has a realistic sense of what one desires to achieve and how much one is willing to pay for it. One can now enjoy a more contented, if more limited, vision of the world, and one can hope (it is never guaranteed) for a peaceful and meaningful life, with time and health to enjoy the fruits of one's labors.

So enjoy your coming birthday and understand that every milestone brings its own unique rewards. You are now old enough to begin to understand yourself and your parents and to have compassion for those who have not matured as well as you did.

We are proud of you and grateful to you. Not just because you have been such a good daughter (you always were that), but because, in this terrifying world for parents, you have avoided many of the perils that have shattered the lives of children of our friends.

I do not envy you the world as it is changing for you and yours. You still have to sweat out the growth and development of your children in a world filled with turmoil and fearful perils that did not exist when we carried your burdens.

Yet, despite this, at forty you are in the full vigor of health, a matured personality and mind, with enough experience to know what you want, need and enjoy. So look ahead. The best is yet to come—if you have the courage and the strength to grasp it.

With love,
Dad

Déjà Vu

Back in the dim past of 1963, when I was a mere lad of eight, my father, Milton, decided to write a book about America. In order to give back something to the country that had so welcomed him as an immigrant child, he wanted to write a book of praise for the land he loved.

The thread of this opus was to be "Gordon Sees America," in which I would be photographed in living color in a profusion of well-known scenic spots all across the country. Suitable text to accompany the photos would be provided by my father.

He approached several publishers with his fine idea and all expressed a remarkable lack of interest in it. They wanted to see the finished product before they made any commitment. Then, maybe, they might consider it as a possibility.

With this firm commitment in hand, my father, my mother and I packed our luggage, loaded the cameras, bought a new car and let it roam the continent with us. It was during this trip that I discovered my interest in cars. I counted all of the just introduced Thunderbirds on the road, reaching the meticulously kept total of 1,234 noted in 60 days.

It was a glorious summer. I was photographed aiming a cannon on Old Ironsides, feeding squirrels in Muir Woods, on a stagecoach in Durango, on Pike's Peak, in Disneyland, in front of Niagara Falls, checking out the Great Divide, holding up the Washington Monument, wearing a costume in Williamsburg, in

Bryce Canyon, in the Grand Canyon, on a mule, on a horse, on a railroad steam locomotive, with a buffalo, looking at alligators, in front of a great Sequoia, at the Air Force Academy in Colorado Springs, on the Strip in Las Vegas, grinding corn in the Mesa Verde, fishing on Cape Cod and walking on the Golden Gate bridge. Also looking at fossilized dinosaur bones in Utah, picking up souvenirs in the Petrified Forest, pushing Boulder Damn, throwing a snowball made of snow found in July in the Rockies, in front of the witch trees of Monterey, in front of a multitude of unusual buildings, natural bridges, mesas, buttes, and just plain rocks. I don't know how many rolls of film my dad shot, but I was getting quite weary of constantly posing.

I really saw the United States as few children ever get the chance. Once, while driving through the beauties of Monument Valley, we all spontaneously burst into singing "America the Beautiful." I've never gotten over the impression of the grandeur and vastness of our country.

However, the point of this lengthy introduction was the eerie event that took place when we drove into Utah. As I've said, the trip, while generally planned, was flexible enough in terms of time and space to let us wander off the beaten paths to pursue any whim or interest any of us had. So without any knowledge of the town, we entered Kanab, Utah, on our way to somewhere else.

As we entered the dusty town, it was, like most days on that wonderful trip, a brilliantly sunny day. The small town was fairly deserted in the shimmering heat of the day.

My father suddenly said, "I know this town. I've been here before."

My mother laughed. "You're crazy. You've never been in Utah before in your life."

"I know that," countered my father, "but I still have the strong feeling that I've seen this town before."

"You just think you do, because it resembles other towns you have visited and it gives the same impression," responded my mother.

"You may be right," said Dad, "but I can tell you what is on the next block. There is a feed and grain store, then a lady's clothing store, a bank, and then a livery stable with a corral."

As the car cruised slowly down the street, we saw just what my father had predicted, the feed and grain store, clothing store, bank and livery stable, in the same order as my father had stated.

My mother was startled. "Did you see this in a dream perhaps?"

"I don't think so," said Dad. "This is creepy, because I know this block as well as I know the shops on our main street at home."

He continued, "I know the next block, too. It has a sheriff's office, a jail and a saloon called The Long Branch."

As the car proceeded down the street, each item appeared as predicted by my father. The name of the saloon, The Long Branch, was the clincher—that was too much for just a vague dream. This was true déjà vu, the feeling that one has undergone a prior experience identical to the one happening now.

Had my father been in this unchanging town in a previous life? Had he a double who lived his life in this town while my father lived another life in Great Neck? Was my father blessed with second sight? Was this an example of the type of stories one encountered in the *National Enquirer?*

My parents discussed the various possibilities, with my father proposing several causes of this phenomenon while my mother skeptically discarded all of them. But she could not respond when he asked, "Okay, if you reject all of my ideas, how do you think I knew all of these things then? I'm not trying to trick you. I'm as puzzled as you are."

Then my father finally turned to me and asked, "What do you think, Gordon?"

I timidly offered, "It looks like Gunsmoke to me. You know, where Marshal Dillon lives."

There was a stunned silence. Then both of my parents burst into hilarious laughter. It was true. We had inadvertently come upon the shooting set for the most popular Western TV show in history. It was no wonder that my father knew the place. He had visited it every week for years, with Festus, Doc and Miss Kitty.

That settled the matter of déjà vu and we had a great laugh. We often fondly recall our memory of Kanab, but somehow I was sorry that my father didn't have a wonderful talent like second sight or the ability to see the future.

My Father Is a Jewish Mother

Most Jewish boys are blessed with a Jewish mother who worries about what they eat, whom they date, how their careers will turn out, and if they come home late. I have been doubly blessed because I have two! My father, Milton, is the archetypical Jewish mother.

He is constantly advancing food on me and he is the only one in our family who ever made me breakfast. His constant refrain, which sounds suspiciously like that of a Jewish mother, is "Eat something." His remedy for almost any ailment is "eat something" or "drink more orange juice, especially when you have a cold."

He is a chronic worrier, especially in matters relating to me, my health, my social life, my job, my clothes, my insurance, my car, the weather, driving conditions, and on and on and on.In short, he worries about everything I do and everything I don't do.

His constant questions start with "Did you..." followed by any number of endings: write to your aunt, call your sister, pay your utilities, take out the garbage, buy a particular stock, and a million other things.

My father is persuaded that the world is filled with malevolent demons, maniacs driving on the highway, thieves watching for the unwary, viruses planning to engulf me, investments ripening to go sour, and folly and vanity waiting to bankrupt one.

So he tries to exorcise these demons and my protect my life and limb by warning me against them. "Take care, take care." Or, in his mother tongue, "*gib achtung.*" His repetition of "be careful" is almost sure to drive me to distraction.

Yet my father was never the nebbish one would associate with the term "Jewish mother." He is a strong, successful and busy man. But he is able to find a tremendous amount of time to worry about me. But life isn't always grim and earnest with my father. He likes to laugh and we've had wonderful times together. He laughs at himself very easily and he is far more tolerant of my foibles than his stern father was of his.

While my father could laugh, when it came to me, he could be as fierce as a tiger. I recall two incidents. Once he slammed the car door on my hand and rushed me to a local surgeon. When the doctor treated me callously and painfully, my father struck him. On another occasion, one of the school bullies, much older than I, gave me a bloody nose without cause. My father visited his father. There was a brief conversation, and the bully avoided me for the rest of the school year.

When my father visits my new apartment and "helps" me with the purchase and placement of the furniture, his advice is always good and always I reject it. After three minutes of his visit, I am back to being six years old again. So, to maintain my adult integrity, I stubbornly resist his suggestions and I do my own thing, even though I realize that it is often wrong. No matter how hard I work cleaning up, it never meets his or my mother's Jewish mother standards.

When I visit my parents' home, my father is usually the one who prepares the meal and offers me food, as well as advice, serious comments, jokes and more food. It is his fault, I claim, that I am getting fat.

He usually is the one who will say, "Are you tired?" or "Why did you work this late today?" or "Do you have a date?" He also will proffer several decorative items, none of which I really desire, that he thinks I could use in my apartment. Rather than argue about them, as I did in the past, I find the better part of valor is to take them and put them away in one of my closets and hope that he will not spot them on his next inspection. When he does, he doesn't yell, but, even worse, he looks hurt.

He also is the one who worries when I am late. He is not above calling my office if I am more than an hour late coming home. He will call the police, the hospitals and the highway patrol if I am more than two hours late. In one story my father tells, he laughingly describes how his parents went out to look for him in a blizzard when he was late coming home from an evening college course. Yet he behaves the same way himself.

Despite my constant refrain not to worry about me and his promise not to worry, the scenario is repeated regularly. When I lived at home, I never came home, no matter how late the hour, without finding my father awake. He would excuse his being up by claiming that he needed to finish some book or article of outstanding interest.

So, in spite of my resistance, my father trained me to call home. I rarely neglect to call home when I know I am going to be delayed more than a half hour. It is easier than dealing with the worried call on my answering machine and easier emotionally than dealing with my guilt when I know that, despite my innocence, I have caused my father real anguish.

He is not trying to smother me. He desperately wants me to get married and find happiness. He is truly worried because I am his greatest grief and his chief joy. He does not spare himself because he is trying to do his utmost for me, but I really wish he would stop. Yet I know that he cannot.

We are both victims of our history. Perhaps my father became a Jewish mother because of his own sickly youth and my difficult birth. His medical history as a child was fraught with pain and peril, so he has projected his fears onto me. He never seemed to worry about my sister, but I was a two-pound preemie and the only surviving son of several unfortunate pregnancies that ended in miscarriages. There definitely would be no more children after me. So all of my father's hopes and fears seemed wrapped up in my then frail person. He paid undue attention to my survival.

Strangely enough, despite my poor early start, I grew like a horse and had few childhood ailments. So maybe that proves something.

My mother, thank God, while often probing in her questions, is less apt to worry with the same intensity that my father applies to the job. I often tell him he worried about many things that never happened. "See," he says, "it works! By my worrying, I am protecting the whole family from disasters they do not worry about."

My father comes by his avocation most honorably. His father was even worse, the world's worst—or best—worrier. My grandfather, who collected disasters instead of stamps, would frequently call my father, then running an organization of thousands of employees, to advise him that:

It was raining or snowing or just plain hot or cold.

It would be a good idea to wear rubbers.

There was a terrible auto accident in Ohio, or Texas, or a ferry capsized in Hong Kong and a hurricane raged in Florida.

It would be a good idea to gib achtung driving to work.

I am not certain how my father felt about this gratuitous advice, because he always respectfully answered his father with a "Yes, Pappa" and then proceeded to ignore the warnings.

I find it a bit more difficult. First, because I am not as strong as my father is in resisting his father's omnipresent influence. I love him so much that I really don't want him to worry. Secondly, I made the mistake of moving back home for a brief time, after having lived in freedom in Boston for seven years. So I received a double dose of childhood training.

My father means well. He is more than generous when it comes to money. Every thought and every effort on my behalf is designed to assist me in coping with life and advancing myself and my career. And it is making me crazy and making me fat.

So I ask the world at large: Does any one of you need an extra mother? Would you adopt one of mine—please?

In The School System

Life as a Tweeny

In the last few decades people have mistaken me for an intellectual. They have been wrong. I never disabused them of the flattering evaluation, but I always knew that their estimate of me was exaggerated. I am really a "tweeny."

Blinded by my glib articulate tongue, confused by my doctorate and my profession, impressed by my role as editor of *The Light,* my synagogue's magazine, most of my friends assumed I was an intellectual. Far from it. I have known real intellectuals in my time—professors who illuminated my mind; people like Rabbi Waxman and his wife, who guided my spiritual growth; fellow students who challenged everything I said. Many of these people were and are giants of the mind.

The term tweeny goes back to my years as a Social Studies teacher in a junior high school in Forest Hills, Queens. There, through political machinations and sheer good luck, 1 was assigned the task (the joy) of teaching a class of the gifted, a super Special Progress (S.P.) class.

Having come from teaching in Bedford Stuyvesant, or BedSty, where I faced gray dreary days of plodding, undisciplined and hostile minds, I was suddenly facing eager, bright, motivated minds that absorbed all I could offer like hungry sponges. All of the material I planned for in my lessons melted like snowballs in a furnace. A week's plan in Bed-Sty lasted less than a period here. I had to stretch as a teacher, plan prodigious amounts of material and really look up all facts I thought I knew, because my students challenged me at every turn. Not rudely, but sharply and with quizzical and amused comments. I really learned my craft.

I should point out that to enter these classes a student needed a minimum I.Q. test score of 130 and most of them tested at over 160, with some going completely off the scale. So that although these ninth graders were between 13 and 15 years old, 1 could offer them college-level lectures withoutt baffling them. They were a wonderful group of students. Many were the children of foreign ambassadors from the United Nation's local housing enclave, as well as children of famous entrepreneurs, politicians and authors, and most were well travelled.

There seemed no task they wouldn't do. They would build beautiful dioramas to illustrate a unit. They would write wonderful final reports and bind them in attractive covers. They would make murals and write plays and poems. One group even wrote an original graduation march for the assembly, and several students rehearsed secretly just to perform this surprise for their parents and fellow students. Despite the stereotype of the genius as short, withdrawn and wearing glasses, 1 found that the students in gifted classes were generally taller, better looking and more social than average students.

Teaching them was like trying to catch sparks in a butterfly net. Their minds and interests soared and swooped. Everything interested them: stars and dinosaurs; Chaucer and Charlie Chaplin; Vikings and vineyards. I could deliver a lecture called "Folk Explosions," dealing with mass migrations of peoples like the Mongols, the Huns, the Vikings and the Crusaders and find that they were with me the whole way.

One day I was surprised by a sudden visit by the school

principal and the superintendent of the district. Since it was Monday and I had spent the weekend working at my summer camp, I was unprepared. So I called on Levine to give his committee report on Columbus. (I called them all by their last names, which pleased them because it reminded them of the English public schools. I also did it because I had great trouble remembering their first names.) Levine then led his committee through a series of superb presentations on the social, economic, military and religious factors that initiated and sustained Columbus' explorations. It was an amazing tour de force that left my supervisors flabbergasted. I was impressed, but I had seen my geniuses in action before. I was given a poor evaluation by the supervisors who felt I should have participated more in the lesson.

Despite their brilliance, they were kind and generous to me. They liked me because I was relaxed with them and gave them their heads as long as they were working. It was a happy class, but my principal complained that there was too much laughter coming from my room.

At Christmas time they showered me with gifts and I loved to accept them. Once when they asked what to get me, I offered the silly suggestion that I could use a money tree. The next day a small evergreen tree appeared on my desk, all covered with U.S. currency. It taught me to watch my mouth with these precocious pupils. When my son was born, they flooded our home with furniture and clothing for the baby. The gifts were far less important to me than what they meant in out relationship. I feel sorry for any teacher who has not had at least one class like that in his or her career.

Since I liked them so much, I often stayed after school to conduct club activities for them. In those days, such service was voluntary and unpaid. Despite the many pressures of other lessons as well as after-school classes in dance and Hebrew andthe all pervasive orthodontia sessions, they showed up for my chess and drama clubs.

While I was a reasonably competent chess player, I never won a game from any of my club members. In desperation I challenged ten of them to ten games simultaneously. Each student sat in a different room while I walked back and forth among them, playing my pieces quickly and brilliantly. I won five and lost five games. My students were amazed. How could I carry the moves for ten complex games in my head? Then they realized that I was not playing those games. I had paired my opponents and I was simply moving back and forth duplicating the moves the opposite number had made. The students were really playing each other, hence I had to win half of the games. That episode became the basis for a lesson on fraud and deception which was as valuable a lesson for my brilliant but often trusting pupils as any I ever taught them.

I realize that I have been privileged to nurture a true national asset, the minds of our best and brightest. Inadvertently, perhaps intuitively, I had developed a free yet industrious and stimulating environment in which they relaxed and flourished. In all of my later professional years I sought to develop programs for gifted classes, but I never could duplicate the excitement and pleasure I got from my S.P. classes. I have always known that money invested in programs for the gifted has great return. These are the students who will some day cure our cancers, speak to the stars and develop the towering philosophies and formulas of the future. But I never could convince the decisionmakers of my point of view, except for some token efforts.

After several years at the school, I made the stupid decision to move up on the supervisory ladder and leave my classes. The pupils graciously threw a farewell party to mark my promotion and sad departure. One of the girls, the spokesperson, thanked me for my efforts and toasted me as her favorite tweeny. I noticed that many of the others smiled, so I knew the strange term had meaning to them. So I asked, "What is a tweeny?"

Hesitantly and without arrogance she said, "We all know that we are smarter than most people and that most of the other students resent us 'brights.' Even other teachers don't like us because we make them nervous with our questions and chatter. But you are different because you are relaxed with us. You are between the 'brights' and the 'stupids'—a tweeny."

After I recovered from the shock of that evaluation, I realized that it was correct. I may not be a stupid but I certainly wasn't a true bright. I was grateful because to be accepted and loved by these remarkable children was an accolade to be cherished.

I am a tweeny and proud to announce it.

Teachers In the Golden City

After attending a warm discussion at the temple about growing up Jewish in New York City and then reading the brief section in Howe's book *World of Our Fathers* dealing with Jewish children in public schools, I wondered: How did it fare with Jewish teachers? When did Jewish teachers appear on the scene? How did the scene change as they appeared?

Although the great Jewish flood from eastern Europe to the *Goldene Medina,* the Golden City, started in the late 1870s, it was not until about 1900 that there were any Jewish teachers in the New York City school system. In fact, by 1906, when more than one-third of the pupils in the New York City schools were Eastern Jews, only 6% of the teachers were Jewish.

In a sense, the Jews are the success story of the public school system, in New York at least. From a rejected and poverty-stricken background, the Jews chose the path of education, usually through the public schools, as their route to middle class status. And they succeeded far beyond any other group, except the Japanese, in using the public schools and free universities to catapult into middle class status within one or two generations. In fact, the Jews really captured the public school system because they played the game according to the rules set up by the school system itself.

While most of the Yankee and Irish teachers tended to look down on their noisy immigrant pupils, they were really not anti-

Semitic, just anti-foreign, applying their bias with equal disdain to the Italians, Greeks, Poles and immigrant Irish. Teachers, with their recently acquired establishment status, looked with mild horror at the noisy, dirty and unteachable rabble deposited in their neat classrooms by the pressures in Europe.

The Jewish pupils as a group tended to be more docile and willing than most of the other immigrant groups. The teachers had their own rating scale, bigoted as it sounds, when they said, "The Italians are fair students, but not as good as the Hebrews and not as bad as the Irish."

Since the Jewish pupils went to school under strict injunctions from their parents to learn, because this seemed the most direct route out of the tenements, they were duty bound to obey the teachers. So they sat quietly, losing foreignisms and lauding the "American way" spouted by the teacher in her thoughtless desire to Americanize these benighted foreigners as soon as possible.

The teacher was a strange being to most of them. First, she spoke without an accent, and the children learned very quickly to avoid the greenhorn accent because the teacher did not like it. A degree of self-hatred and alienation from one's parents was part of the price these pupils paid for the assimilation into the melting pot.

The teachers also dressed differently, with skirt and blouse and usually a small watch on the lapel—a being from another planet. It is no wonder the children tried to please her and then to emulate her by becoming themselves that most wonderful being, a teacher. So the children learned and did well in school. After all, they were the "people of the book." A strong family structure was also a help. The Jews tended more than other immigrant groups to emigrate as families, not just single men, as did the Irish and the most rejected of all, the Chinese. Not until the Japanese arrived with the same strong family structure and discipline would another immigrant group have an equally disproportionate number of university graduates in the second generation.

The teachers used their authority and their position as role models to indoctrinate the young students and teach the American way. This often included humiliating the pupils by checking publicly for lice and nits. And many a child would be sent home with instructions in Yiddish and Italian, printed in advance by the authorities, on how to rid the child of these terrible blemishes. It taught a lesson still practiced in many Jewish homes: clean shirts go with good marks, or at least the reverse may be true. So why take a chance?

Most adults received their indoctrination and a large measure of their real education in American ways via the union meeting and the Union Hall. The children were taught every day in school that to appear foreign was to lose out on what America had to offer. They learned to eliminate or at least conceal their immigrant inferiority by assuming American ways and dress as soon as possible. To be an immigrant was no crime but something almost worse: it was an obstacle to a better way of life.

So the children arrived in school neatly dressed, at what cost in labor to the mothers struggling in cold-water flats, and even with ribbons and ties to please the teacher. They behaved well because the teacher detested "excitable" (read noisy) children and they wanted to be liked and accepted by the teachers.

Teachers during the period from 1870 to the turn of the century were usually appointed because of influence, hence the faculty that faced the pupils of the period was completely unrepresentative of the student body in the urban melting pot that was New York City. While most of the pupils were recent immigrants, such as Greeks, Jews, Italians, Poles, and Bohemians, the teachers were usually Yankee, that is, Anglo-Saxon or Irish. In 1906, with 72% of the students of immigrant origin, only 6% of the teachers were Jewish and the other immigrant groups were even more poorly represented. By then there was one solitary Jewish school principal, but there appears to be not even one Italian teacher on the rolls at that time.

Jews, realizing that the role of influence in obtaining teaching positions was against their interest, pressed for a Civil Service approach, where they felt merit and not influence, which they lacked, would be the basic factor in getting employment.

They were largely successful. Once they changed the rules, the number of Jewish teachers increased. In one school, Jewish teachers soon comprised 16 out of a faculty of sixty, and in P.S. 20 on Rivington Street, there were 29 Jewish teachers in a faculty of sixty. The authorities placed immigrant teachers among immigrant pupils. The reason was not to provide a role model for students, however. Since the immigrants were segregated by housing and economics, the Board of Education deliberately continued this policy in its assignment of teachers.

Despite the change to Civil Service, Jews still did not find it easy to become teachers. The Establishment had its own rules, and the path to certification was made difficult. Teachers had to undergo stringent examinations. Not all of these exams were relevant, but they did serve to eliminate the "undesirables." So some Jewish teachers were excluded because of "foreignisms," such as a New York accent, shown by the horrible inadequacy of pronouncing "Long Island" as "Long Guyland." All sorts of esoteric problems were developed to eliminate potential teachers. One brilliant and now extremely successful executive was denied a teacher's license because of a "sibilant 's'." What that had to do with his ability to teach is still a mystery.

Since the rating of examinations and interviews was subjective and not subject to review or appeal, it was easy to drop a Jewish teacher for vague reasons such as "poor scholarship" or "unresponsive to the question." But the Jews persevered, and as the number of Jewish teachers increased, they pushed for other changes.

Unwilling like their predecessors to remain "spinsters," they fought for and obtained the right to be married without loss of their jobs. That in turn forced the Board of Education to adopt regulations on maternity leave, a not suprising result of the previous victory on marital status.

Once there was a sufficient pool of Jewish teachers, it was only a matter of time before there would be more and more Jewish principals. It is true that Julia Richman, a most remarkable woman of Bohemian Jewish background, had not only been appointed a principal in 1884 but in 1903 was made the first woman district superintendent in New York City. Her district? The Lower East Side, of course. But except for a few such unique individuals, it was some time until any major breakthrough took place.

By 1929, almost sixty years after the flood of Jewish immigration started, there were still only six Jewish high school principals. Folklore has it that five had converted to Catholicism in order to obtain their appointments.

Since the route to promotion under the system was by ever more difficult examinations, the Jews studied. Oh, how they studied! Coaching courses and study groups were developed to assist candidates to cope with the lengthy and largely irrelevant and esoteric examination procedures. By the mid-fifties, the examinations for assistant principals could take two to three years and comprised several hours of written essays, hours of short answer questions, a lengthy interview for speech, a long interview for educational information, a practice observation of a teacher at work, a review of records and a physical exam. But despite this, many Jewish teachers took the exams. Many failed, but some passed, until over the years most of the principal positions were held by Jews.

It must be realized that it was not just sufficient to get a passing grade in all parts. One needed a high score in order to be appointed before the list lapsed and it was necessary to start the painful process all over again.

Of course, the holders of power were not anxious to share it with the interlopers. While Jews succeeded in breaking into the ranks of teachers, they were excluded from higher positions. Superintendents were chosen from those in the Old Boys Club and only those in the image of the Establishment were selected. Long after Jews were in a complete majority as teachers and principals, the superindencies, about 50 in all, were held mainly by WASPs and the Irish. It is remarkable that with the multitude of Jewish students, the first Jew to hold the rank of Superintendent of Schools in New York City was not until the mid-1960s, when Calvin Gross held the office for a mere two years, finally followed by Irving Anker, who served for a year in 1970 and then for five years starting in 1973.

Even when Jewish pressure on the lower ranks of the district superintendencies became great, it was still the custom to allocate the vacancies on a rotating basis: one Jewish superintendent, one Catholic, and then one Protestant, and then around again. And the Jews took it. They played the game even though others had developed the rules, and they took over and improved the system despite all obstacles.

And keep in mind that there were no bilingual programs when Jewish students started, at a time when almost every immigrant child in the system was bilingual. You made it or you dropped out. The system did not really care. It was grateful for the empty seat because the establishment was niggardly in erecting new and expensive schools in the slums and tenements.

In the 1970s we could look back and see that the Jews had climbed the mountain and made it theirs. But then it turned into a volcano, as new groups of Hispanic immigrants and black students sought to use the school system as their springboard to middle class status—but not by taking irrelevant exams and waiting a generation. They wanted jobs and status sooner than that. By strenuous agitation, demonstrations and the efforts of the civil rights movement, and often with the support of Jews, they achieved some of their goals in less time than the Jews did.

As the new contenders pressed in, the Jews moved out, some to retirement and others to the suburbs. And as these new strivers had often been taught by Jewish teachers, one could say that Jews trained, matured and supported the groups that supplanted them.

Observations and Commentary

A Kluge Zu Columbus

In less than ten years, this nation, along with all of Latin America, will engage in a paroxysm of celebrations commemorating the 500th anniversary of the "discovery" of America by Christopher Columbus. While the indigenous population hates the demeaning term "discovery" because they had flourishing civilizations here before the Europeans accidentally intruded on their turf, the general population will tell the tale of the great discovery made by those who were really seeking the land of Silk, Spices and Sony.

This celebration will coincide with the 100th anniversary of the decade that was the high point in the wave of Eastern European migration to the United States. This coincidence brings to mind a phrase, in decline now, that was constantly on the lips of my East New York and "Brunzvill" neighbors: *A Kluge Zu Columbus.* It is a phrase that defies accurate translation: A complaint to Columbus? An indictment of Columbus? It is all Columbus' fault? May Columbus be cursed? It was all of these, plus. It was a comment made in despair, in confusion, in regret, in anger. It was a wry bit of advice similar to the army suggestion to take your problems to the Chaplain. What can one do in this mad and different and indifferent land? That attitude is inextricably bound and wrapped in the phrase. It was both a release and a provocation when it was uttered.

What it tries to express is the concept that if Columbus had not stumbled on this "new land," there would have been no mass migrations and so no hordes of self-displaced persons struggling to adjust to a new and very often hostile environment.

True that life in the *shtetl,* the Jewish ghetto, was poor and grim, full of fear, discrimination, and poverty, along with prejudice and pogroms as constant irritants and terrors. But these were familiar demons that could be countered and held at bay by the warm circle of family relations and the stability of knowing your "proper" place in the traditional scheme of things. Tradition, while stultifying to personal freedom, put safe limits on personal aberrations and interpersonal conduct, manners and conversations. While being Jewish was difficult, there was no other choice except for apostasy, with its severing of all family and community connections. So most people adhered to the community's established standards of behavior.

But in America, A Kluge Zu Columbus, everything was different. The clothing was different, the food tasted different, even the shape and color of the sky was different. The clouds, hidden from view in the concrete canyons, were dreary and grey, where once they had been like white marble one could cut steps into. While the streets were paved, (though not with gold) and were not filled with the *blutte* [mud] of the village streets, here they were filled with noise, debris and shameful stenches.

Whether one had once lived in a hovel or a comfortable many-roomed brick house, at least it was the home of one family. Here one was crowded into the few rooms of a flat, sharing toilet facilities with several families. These apartments were lightless, freezing in the winter and suffocating during the sweltering summers, but always noisy and redolent of many mingled cooking odors. And the *lendler,* the landlord, was the constant enemy.

But the housing, once obtained, was easier to cope with than the new language, with its weird rules of pronunciation and spelling and with a grammar that seemed to follow no logical premise. Every rule seemed to have more exceptions than cases governed by the rule. What could you do with a language that spelled "though" and "enough" the same, but pronounced them so differently? Then try to explain "through!" Tough and dispiritng as well to untangle "to," "too," and "two" while striving to make a living.

The sense of dislocation, of anonymity and alienation, was so intense that it drove many to despair. The loss of the familiar streets, of parents and siblings, of aunts and cousins, of Rabbi and synagogue, even of the burial ground, was keenly felt and only partly compensated for by the fierce attachment to *landsleit,* fellow countrymen who settled nearby in the new country. The societies and organization formed by these landsleit were clung to for a shred of sanity and protection in the shifting sands of change. A Kluge Zu Columbus: I had to give up the security and familiar faces of home for this *meshugas,* this craziness?

Seeking a livelihood in a land where old skills and traditional status had no value was terrifying and traumatic. A Yeshivah education was worse than useless. It became a hindrance and source of mockery. It was better to be a *gruber yung,* a coarse fellow, with strength or sales ability. The latter could *drey* and *drey,* work and work, and become an "alrightnik" doing well in his own business. The scholar was grateful that someone loaned him a sewing machine so he could, for meager wages, cough out his lungs in a sweatshop, *A Bruch,* a blessing, Zu Columbus.

But the worst was the topsy-turvy changes in the roles of the generations. *Der Futter*, the papa, was often no longer the respected head of the family. The children, learning English like summer lightning, made fun of the parents' inarticulate and heavily accented English. Able to use the schools to move into the *goyishe* [non-Jewish] world with greater ease, they felt constrained by, and contempt for, the old standards. "This is America, Papa" became a constant charge of inadequacy and unreasonable adherence to useless values on the part of the parents and the excuse for any excess in dating, dress and deportment.

And so, A Kluge Zu Columbus, the move towards acculturation and assimilation started with a wrenching loss to the parents. Not only had they left their parents behind, their own children were now leaving them behind. *Streimels* [fur hat] and *shaitels* [wigs] and *payes* [side curls] as well as accents, names and noses were discarded in the desperate race to be a "Yenkey," to make a living, and to gain acceptance and status. With the rise in their levels of aspiration came the jettisoning of much of the ritual and standards and paraphernalia that they had brought from Europe.

The very freedom that the parents had sought for their children seduced their children from them. "You can be anything you want in America" became the siren song of rejection. Anything, that is, but a proper respectful obedient child. Why, girls selected their own "fellers," made dates, and went dancing, and—A Kluge Zu Columbus—even decided whom they would marry!

So at the cost of several generations of shattering psychological conflict, the Jews "discovered" the *Goldene Medina*, the Golden City, of Columbus and succeeded beyond their

wildest dreams. From shtetl to state house in one genera-
tion; from poor *greena kocker* [green horn] to prosperous
business *knocker* [big shot]; from Talmud *chacham* [wise man] to
Columbia Ph.D. None of these were unusual transformation.
They surged from the East Side to the Bronx, to Scarsdale, to
Great Neck, in fifty years.

The union hall, the theater, the public schools, all became
the centers of learning and the places in which to gain status and advancement. The schools inculcated the American
ideal by making children ashamed of their heritage. The Beth
Hamidrash and the Talmud Torah, the religious schools, were
sentimental vestigial organizations that were supported to avoid
giving fuel to the gossips. "What would the neighbors say" was
really a plea to the children to conform, at least outwardly, to
the old standards and not shame the parents. The plea was usually disregarded because of the young peoples' impatience to
conform to the new standards.

So sang the song of the seductive society: buy our values
and behave like us and all doors are open unto you. You will be
free to grow and free to get and free to amass honors and
degrees. America was the first free society for the Jews since
the expulsion from Spain (also in that same fateful year of
1492) and the Jews reveled in it. At the cost of being sanitized
and homogenized in the melting pot, the Jews were not overtly
excluded from everything.

The Pledge of Allegiance, chanted lustily to please the Irish
spinster teacher, that envied role model, made the sacred prayer
Sh'ma Yisrael seem even more foreign and exotic to the ears
of the children. Anything foreign was a detriment and every
vestige of the old country was an albatross forever miring you
in the despised Hester Street.

While the drift away from strict adherence to Jewish ritual and behavior had been started in Europe and imported here, the trend was accelerated in America. The pattern established by the earlier arrivals, the German Jews, of not observing the Sabbath and limiting overt religiosity was deemed the appropriate model to follow by those who were ambitious and eager to follow the road to acceptance in America.

The very tight housing itself contributed to the dissolution of the family because it forced the youngsters to congregate in the streets, where a street corner youth culture further eroded the old traditions and authority. Peer pressure led to crime and other asocial activities and, at the very least, to an abandonment of Jewish values and deportment.

The fathers were also deprived of the support of the older generations that they had left behind. They had lost the line of continuity from the old country and the authority derived from the established way of doing things.

The Jews very intense desire for education led to the loss of parental status as the public library, with its many volumes on so many diverse topics, became the basic source of ideas and values to the younger generation. In any clash between the two value systems, the glitter and fluency and American merit of the books won out over the desperate and often inarticulate demands of the parents. A Kluge Zu Columbus. *Mi ken nur veinen*—one can only cry.

Everything American was to be admired. How I longed to be a steely grey-eyed rider of the purple sage, who looked lean and lanky like Gary Cooper and said, "Yup." I looked into the mirror and saw, like most of my friends, a pudgy, brown-eyed, "Jewish looking" boy, and I despaired. To look "unJewish" was an asset to be cherished and admired. If you couldn't do that, at least you could stop "acting Jewish." Self-hatred was the price one or more generations paid so that our children could be accepted into Ivy League schools. Maybe "black is beautiful," but early in this century, swarthy was definitely out. While most of the heroes were blond and tall, the villains in literature were usually dark and spoke with foreign accents. All swarthy people were suspected of evil, or at least dissolute ways. To look like a "shiftless gypsy" was the ultimate insult and cause for anxiety for one's career and marital status.

So the Jews became Americans, but, A Kluge Zu Columbus, were they still Jews? Fewer than half belonged to any synagogue or Jewish organization. A token attendance at a Yiskor or Kol Nidre service seemed to suffice, because the United Jewish Appeal and the B'Nai Brith seemed more significant than the temple. Intermarriage, birth control, cult membership and simply drifting away from Jewish roots, ideas and rituals were eroding the only significant surviving Diaspora community.

But grateful for the stubborn fortitude and strength of purpose that enabled their once-rejected grandparents to lift them out of the path of the Nazi juggernaut and the ovens of the Holocaust, this third generation of Jews showered support and praise upon the phoenix of Israel. Even with the rise of anti-Semitism as the guilt for the Holocaust recedes and the influence of the Arabs rises, one can see hopeful signs.

New temples are spreading far and wide to replace those left behind in the decaying inner cities. Jewish education for children and adults is increasing. The search for Jewish roots and the temporary resurrection of Yiddish are indications that there is still vigor among the B'nai Israel, the children of Israel.

Seminary enrollment is increasing and the depth and breadth

of the curriculum has grown. The Jews have a strong influence, even if not power, in the media, in literature, and in many professions, in sharp contrast to the early days. The ability of Jews to mount fierce and often effective campaigns and demonstrations when Jewish or Israeli interests are threatened is a sign of a vigorous community. The White House maintains liaisons with the major Jewish organizations and no serious political candidate ignores the Jewish community during his campaign. It is clear that Congress is responsive to Jewish lobbying. It is also clear that the surreptitious cajoling of "court Jews" has been supplanted by a well organized and closely linked network prepared to rouse the body politic with public outcries. It would be impossible for the Holocaust, or even an indecent incident like the turning away of the refugee ship St. Louis during World War II, to occur, without a terrible outcry from the Jewish community and its political allies.

Best of all, many of the younger generation are opting for establishing religious, even kosher, homes and appear to be completely unself-conscious about being Jews. The burgeoning Havurah movement of small, Jewish fellowship groups and the solidarity of the Hassidic communities are good signs that we can look forward to a vigorous Jewish community.

The forms may be different—and why should there not be new forms? After all, there is no large or significant Jewish community that exists in the same place that it existed 100 years ago. As the lands and languages change, so there must be adjustments. These adjustments, even with errors and excesses, are tributes to the vitality and flexibility of our people as new norms and new forms rise to cope with changing conditions.

These forms will differ from our forms as our forms differed from those of our ancestors, but the essence, the spirit, will survive and flourish. So we can look forward to 1992, when we can join the celebration and cry out our thanks to this sweet land that let us in. A land that promised much, and delivered much, to our people. *A Leben Uf Columbus*—Long Life Columbus!

Aurora Borealis: Glory on High

When you are raised in and live in the city, you rarely look up at the sky, especially at night. The buildings block out all but a narrow arc of the heavens and the lights blot out the frail glimmer of the stars. Night lights in the city are really signs, traffic lights, advertising displays, and so on, not the natural glow of heavenly bodies. One is kept to the viewing angle of a worm.

One of the most stirring events in my life was the night I really saw the heavens and their most stupendous display. I realized then that, except for some toying with astronomy, I had never really looked up or seen the stars before.

At our summer camp, high in the Catskill mountains, the stars were usually clear, sharp and brilliant because they didn't need to compete with the artificial glow of city lights. Late one August night, about two a.m., I heard the murmuring of many voices on the lawn in front of the directors' cottage. When I came out to investigate, I saw about 30 counselors and senior campers raptly looking up at the northern sky.

There was a magnificent curtain of flickering, silver light extending across the entire horizon. The whole sky seemed alive, pulsating and glowing. I was awe-struck. I had never seen anything like it before.

"What is it?" I asked. The student counselors attending college always knew everything, even when they didn't.

"Shh," said the head counselor, as though afraid a loud voice would shatter the cascading display of light. "It's the northern lights, the aurora borealis."

"Oh, the northern lights," I thought. I knew what that was. I had taught geography in the city schools and knew about this phenomenon. I had even lectured about the effect of solar flares exciting the atoms on the surface of the earth's atmosphere, which caused this scintillating display of emitted light. I had used the banal phrase "similar to static electricity." I had spoken about ionization and the conversion of energy into light. But all of these were just words, weak symbols designed to limit and trap true majesty. How inadequate and puerile these words were to describe the wonder I was viewing now!

My soul was caught up in the shimmer, the constant, yet ever-changing movement, the folding, the unfolding, the dancing drapery, the iridescent and luminous qualities of the light that played across the sky. It was a white fire against a black sky. Like Moses' bush, it burned without fuel or ash.

While there were some blocks of color, the shifting intensities of light, sparkling and shining, was mostly various shades of silver, white and black. God's Art Deco was on display. He flaunted it to show man His signs and wonders and show how small man and the earth were in His scheme of things. From His high and holy place, He sent down arrows and spears of silver fire to magnify and sanctify His name.

I was enthralled by the sight and impressed by the wondrous silence. Displays in the sky are usually accompanied by the boom of rockets, the crackle of fireworks and the crowd's loud exclamations of "Ooh!" and "Ah!" But as we watched the ballet of light, glowing swirlings and wavings like a vast toreador's cape, we were absolutely quiet.

Even the usually boisterous campers were quiet and absorbed, limiting their conversations to muffled "Oohs." No shouts, no laughter, just smiles and soft pleasure. Each knew that this was something very special, that we were being made privy to one of God's treasures and were viewing a true mystery. It was as if we were looking into the creation itself or into the atom. It was as though a sigh had been frozen into light. Were these souls on fire or angels passing by?

I felt the raw, frozen silence of empty inter-stellar space. There was a sense of danger, such as is inherent in an unmoving glacier or a glittering iceberg. But the soundlessness was not frightening. It was a calming silence, with the slightest touch of menace, that reached deep into me. I suddenly knew what was meant by the terms "trailing Robes of Glory" and "the radiance of the foot of God's throne."

I had not seen God, but like the wings of the wind, I had seen God's passing-by. The sky was a temple and our mountaintop had become an altar, as the heavens held a service to honor God, a ceremony of praise through lights.

For hours we stood and gazed, murmuring and silent, as our eyes filled with the grace and glory of the All Highest, a vision of a portion of the throne of the Lord.

Finally, cold, tired and humbled, we all went to bed. As I entered my cottage, I looked back to feast once more on the splendid, shining, pulsating curtain of brilliant and mysterious lights, and reluctantly went in. It was a special and unique moment.

Many times since, I've gazed up at the northern sky and felt emptiness as the aurora borealis did not appear on the horizon. The special conditions that had brought the northern lights so far south below the Arctic Circle were rare. I felt the loss and the disappointment, but I was warmed by the memory of having seen them once, in all their full, pristine glory.

Hair Today

Recently I read about a barbershop in Beirut being bombed by an Islamic fundamentalist group because it wanted to stop the spread of western decadence. I thought, "Is even a haircut a political statement now?"

Then I realized that hair, the way it is cut or displayed, is a powerful statement, a statement of vast cultural, religious, sexual or political significance that goes back to the earliest history of our race.

Throughout different eras, hairstyles reflected the status and often the political leanings of the wearer. In ancient Egypt, the lower classes are always depicted with shaven heads, presumably as a defense against the omnipresent vermin. But the Pharaoh is always shown wearing a head covering to protect him from the fierce rays of Ra, the sun god. And even on the walls of Egyptian tombs, the different races of prisoners—Nubian, Habiru, Philistine—are carefully defined by different hairstyles

The Chinese queue, or pigtail, plays an important role in history. It was initiated by the northern Mongol, or Manchu, conquerors, who insisted that the Chinese wear it as a symbol of their subjugation. Immediately upon the "Ten Ten Ten" revolution of October 10, 1910, these queues were joyfully cut off as a symbol of new-found freedom.

In Cromwell's time in England, the elegantly bewigged Royalists were defeated by the Round Heads with their bowl-shaped haircuts. When Dr. Ben Franklin appeared at the French court amid the powdered wigs of the aristocrats, he was lauded as a true revolutionary because he wore his own unpowdered hair. The Jacobins who also disdained powdered wigs soon removed the wigs of the aristocrats—and their heads, using the ultimate barber, Madame Guillotine.

The Russian "programniks" and the Nazis who cut or tore off the beards of Jews were venting their spite and hatred for what they considered an alien symbol. On the other hand, Kemal Ataturk forced all of the Turks to shave off their beards as a way to kick his countrymen into the 20th century, against their will. It is no accident that Khomeni and the others of the fundamentalist ilk go around looking like unkept hair mattresses. It is interesting to note that to the proudly clean-shaven Greeks and Romans, the barbarians, based on the word for beard, were considered ignorant savages because they were not clean-shaven.

In caricature, hair is one way to define nationality, as one can see by the stereotyped braids of Gretchen, the square hair cut of the Dutch Boy, the beard of the Frenchman compared to the unbearded John Bull, and of course the sinister pointed beard of the Spanish Grandee. It is no accident that the Devil is usually portrayed wearing the pointed Van Dyke beard of the sophisticated seducer or that in the United States the Bolshevik bomb thrower was depicted as a wild figure with a bushy black beard.

Even the color and position of hair has significance. Until recently, no woman except a harlot would wear her hair dyed. No woman would appear in public with her hair unbound. This was deemed lascivious, as a woman's hair could only be seen by her husband in the privacy of the bedroom. Unbound hair was a sign of sexual surrender and only a sinful temptress would indecently display her tresses in public. Decent women wore long hair respectably tied it up in a bun. In fact, all "spinsters" were depicted with buns to indicate the tight and restrained discipline they maintained on their emotions.

A young girl in Edwardian England wore her hair down to indicate she was still considered a child. Wearing her hair up was a signal that she was approaching marriageable age and her hair was to be hidden, reserved for her future husband. Many primitive tribes followed similar customs and had their own signs to show that certain maidens were now approachable.

Hair could also be used as a threat. The infamous pirate Blackbeard wore slow-burning matches in his beard to terrify his enemies. Similar tactics were used by the crested hair Mohawks, the braided Viking Berserker and the wild haired "fuzzy wuzzies" of the Sudan. All of these hairstyles were designed to strike fear in an enemy and mark off a friend in swirling hand-to-hand combat.

Even legends reflect the fear of untamed tresses. Medusa with her wild snake-like locks struck fear in the hearts of the neat and curly-headed Greeks. To wear long and uncombed hair as Medea does is Oriental to the western Greeks, and such a person is doomed from the start in drama.

Religion often emphasizes the symbolic value of hair. The beards and *peyote,* or side curls, of the Orthodox Jews are clear ethnic and religious statements that define their identity and go back to the mystique of the Nazarite with the uncut hair. "And no razor shall come upon his head," says the Torah, because these were holy men sworn to serve God.

The story of the Nazarite Judge Samson who loses his hair and thus his strength (and virility) is still reflected in the shirt which exposes the virile hairy chest of present-day "swingers," who preen themselves before supposedly admiring females.

The use of the hair shirt, which goes back to the ancient prophets and became a feature of the medieval church's desire for self-mortification, is simply another psychological and physiological aspect of the importance of hair.

The covering or uncovering of the hair on the head, as with Orthodox Jewish women, served to define the status of a person. Hence the square beards of the Greek Orthodox Patriarch, the bald-spot tonsure of the medieval monk, and the *shaitel* or wig worn by Orthodox Jewish women, all have religious significance and represent cultural norms that praise God in their different ways.

Our American culture is ambivalent about hair. In early years the settlers were clean-shaven, then beards became popular. Abe Lincoln reluctantly donning a beard (to the point where he does not look like Lincoln to us without a beard) reflects this change. The cartoon Uncle Sam wearing the whiskers of the rural farmer is a symbol of our country. Mustaches can have different connotations. The villain of melodramas curls his mustachio while leering and demanding "the girl or the rent" and is roundly hissed by the audience.

In my mother's day, women cut off "their crowning glory" and adopted the modern boyish bob as an aspect of the war against female bondage and a reflection of the struggle for sexual equality. And in my day, men were supposed to wear their hair short and only a "deviant" or a musician was permitted the luxury of being a "long-hair." In fact, the term "long-hair" was a slur, denoting a freakish interest in art and music. "Real" men wore crew cuts.

My grandfather had a magnificent red beard, but my father was proudly smooth-faced, although he did venture a mustache at one time, and I wear a small beard and mustache—perhaps because in my youth doctors and professors wore neatly trimmed Van Dykes as a sign of learning and these usually elicited respect. All different styles, yet each is a consistent reflection of our times, places and culture.

The political implications of hair continue today. The growth of beards by black men is a rejection of the time all blacks, no matter how old, were denigrated by the term "boy." There is no doubt that the Afro was a political gesture that was emulated by the curly-headed young Jewish liberals who wore a similar style to gain entrance into the ranks of the civil rights movement. The play *Hair* showed the hippie culture of nudity, drugs and sexual promiscuity, a rejection of the middle class values of parents that was symbolized by the rejection of parental hairstyles. It was a rebellion against the materialism of the older generation, whose money and position made their protesting children secure from the consequences of their profligacy and stupidity.

People are still making political statements concerning their ethnic identities and political allegiances by the way they display their hair. Examples abound: the beard of Castro; the nimbus hair of Ben Gurion and Einstein; the unbearded but never clean-shaven visage of Arafat; the shaven pates of the Hari Krishna cultists; the wigs of the English jurists; the sophisticated mustaches of Adolph Menjou and Ronald Coleman; the beehive bouffants of the Kennedy years; the blue-rinsed matrons of Leisure Village; the violent skinheads of Liverpool; the long lanky hair of the blondes in the orange juice commercials. Each is carrying a sandwich board which sets them off from the rest of the world and defines who they are. Each is making a point to instruct or anger or dismay the world. Even the unisex nongenedered hairstyles are a message, presumably for the equality of the sexes.

So hair is a political statement and barbers (pardon me, hairstylists) may be political subversives or patriots depending on your point of view. Hair styles can be a divinely mandated aspect of life, or a logical manifestation of culture and status, or a weird *meshugas* or craziness, depending on your perspective and roots. Show me your hair and I will know whom you reject and who your enemies are. What is your hair saying about you?

Growing Older

Night Sounds

You'd think that a large city hospital is a quiet place at night. The halls are deserted. The gloom seems to absorb all noise. Yet the place resonates with sounds.

Eyes of the ill glow from the darkness of the rooms. The air is full of apologetic calls for aid.

"Help me, help me."

"I'm dying, nurse, I'm dying."

"Bring me something."

Voices are often intermingled as one caller awakens and enrages another patient. Soon a colloquy between two unseen participants, neither knowing the other, takes place.

"Help me, help me."

"Ellen, take me home."

"Shut up, shut up!"

"Give me something."

"Shut up, goddammit "

"Where am I?"

"Nurse, nurse!"

"Help me, help me."

It is like the non-conversation that takes place in an aviary, when each bird screams, setting off another scream, resulting in a wild cacophony. The staff going about their tasks pay no attention to this din of the seriously ill. It is the background noise of the corridors, augmented by the susurration of the oxygen tanks, the bubbling of the IV tubes, the beep-beep of the coronary monitor, the soft chimes of the public-address system and the creak of the waterproof mattress covers as incontinent victims painfully turn over.

Every night the staff changes as the nurses' schedules change. Different, as waves in the ocean are made up of different water, yet all alike. The similarity persists as they quietly sip their coffee, read and write reports, discuss the weather, talk about weekend dates and romances. Laughter surges up often. They are not cruel, just unaware, and habituated to filtering out and ignoring these inessential noises.

The carefully polished hall floors reflect the lights in the corridor. Two lit but soundless TV screens duel across an empty corridor. The white-clad nurses quietly check charts, distribute medications, review instructions left by the supermen called doctors and respond, on occasion, to the call bells on the patients' bedsides.

There are two other sounds: The hard click-clack of nurses' heels as they purposefully stride the corridors; the snap-snick-snack of rubber gloves being put on, as the young doctors pompously pontificate with trite phrases and even faultier understanding of the connection between age, illness and attitudes. Armored in their youth, health and ignorance, they cannot understand the fears of the sick aged.

Nurses hover over and work on patients in lighting similar to the Rembrandt *Autopsy* painting. In the gloom, the semi-alert eyes of a roommate glint back as he silently notes how they work on his partner-in-pain.

Eyes are prominent features of the rooms, one patient notes, as, unsleeping, he walks the halls. The eyes stare at you from the murky depths of the rooms, filled with pain, anger, despair, hostility, envy or a complete lack of interest. Each person is wrapped in his own pains and fears.

Most nurses, whether black, white or Asian, are soft, nurturing and patient, yet steel-strong and authoritative. They move briskly and efficiently among their charges, intuitively allotting their time and attention among the many conflicting claims and demands.

My roommate, once a proud burly man, is dying of advanced emphysema. Every night he rips the oxygen tube out of his throat, tears loose all the catheters, smashes his mask and proceeds to strangle.

I ring and shout for the staff. The nurses and doctors rush in and "rescue" him, despite his savage breathless curses and shouts.

"Get it off, goddammit. I'll kill all of you—you SOBs!"

He tries to strike them. They hold his frail arms, so he uses his tongue as a lash. The nurses, amazingly patient, despite this drama being replayed several times during the night, offer soothing incantations. *"All right, all right. You'll be fine. Relax. This will be over soon."*

They install new equipment, insert new catheters, and bind his wrists to the bars of the bed. He breathlessly rages at me for my interference.

He spends the rest of the night muttering angrily, while working the bonds loose. Sometimes he deliberately holds his breath, but he does not have the strength to solve his problem.

Every day, his tiny, chinless wife tearfully admonishes him for "causing trouble." He curses her and begs God to let him die.

One night, at about eight, I become aware of a loud, hectoring male voice in a neighboring room.

"Try to cooperate. Dammit, eat! You'll be better off. Eat! You must eat."

"You have carrots, you have peas, just the way you like them. What else do you want? Tell me!"

One can hear a soft if unintelligible murmuring female voice, pleading for peace, for some relief from the annoying commands. The harsh hectoring continues unabated.

"I don't want to hear that. Eat! I will not stop until you eat. I don't want to hear about your esophagus. Eat!"

"What did you do now? You dropped it! Come on, I'll sit you up so you can eat better. Please eat!"

This angry tirade continued until 11, when the visitor left the patient to her own peace and her own devices. The next night the entire drama, with the same limited dialogue, took place again. It was repeated the night after that.

Unable to tolerate the noise and the mystery any longer, I made my way from my room, inflamed leg, IV stand and all, to determine the source of this dialog.

I looked into the room and saw a sturdy young man about my son's age, hovering threateningly over a frail woman and angrily shouting, *"What's the matter today, mother? Do you want puffed rice? They have puffed rice, just ask them. Do you want to sit up? What is the complaint now, mother? Eat!"*

He holds a tiny forkful of food before her mouth. Her silent noncompliance results in her eating a small forkful of food for every five minutes of his tirade. She defeats him with a hidden smile and a soft "I can't." Exhausted, he leaves the room and we talk.

"Why don't you leave her alone?" I inquire.

He smiles bitterly at me. "You, too? You think I am cruel to her? Not that it is any of your business, but I am trying to keep her alive. My father died last year and she is my whole family. I am an only child and she has no one else. I have no one else. I won't let her die!"

Slumping against the wall, he continues, "She has cancer of the esophagus and eating is very painful to her. The staff just puts her food in front of her and the whole day goes by without her eating anything. She needs the food to fight the cancer. She can't live on the IV stuff. She is really starving to death and the staff is too busy to care. So I come down here every night from my business two hours away and try to feed her from the trays that are left her. I can't let her die. I can't."

I am shocked by the tragedy and his earnest anger and I regret that I interfered. As an apology, I offer to try to feed her the next day.

He looks at me quietly. "Thanks, but she will not eat from anyone but me. It's her way of knowing how much I love her. But you would relieve my mind a lot if you promise to call me at my business if any problem develops with her."

I look into the room at the pain-wracked face of this frail, almost skeletal woman as she looks at her angry son with warm, loving eyes. I agree to telephone him about any problems with his mother.

Two days later I call to tell him that she no longer needs to be fed. We both cry.

Awaiting the Messenger

He was terribly surprised to see that the sun was shining and that traffic was moving normally. How could that be when his world had been so cataclysmically shattered during the last hour? It was impossible that the world could appear so unchanged, so normal and so unperturbed. When he was so transformed, how could the world be going about its normal, or abnormal, routine, as though nothing significant had occurred?

The doctor had told him, compassionately but quite definitely, that he was very likely to die soon. When he asked whether there were any options for him, the doctor said, "Except for medication and prayer, there is very little we can do for you. Medication may hold off another attack for a while, but it will not change much. Another incident is inevitable soon."

After he absorbed this shocking news, he walked out onto the sidewalk, with all around him going about their own business. In a semi-stunned state, he walked to his car and slowly, almost blindly, drove home.

While the news was shocking, it really wasn't surprising. He had undergone several medical procedures—a nice euphemism for radical and major surgery. He had been keenly aware that he was on a downhill slide, a slide that had been accelerating during the last few months. With each passing week he knew that this pain did not bode well for him. So the doctor simply confirmed what he had feared. He had known for a long time that he was in a precarious position, that he was very, very mortal and that any moment could be his last. The rivers would flow, spring flowers would dance and fruit would ripen, but not for him.

He smiled wryly. He could not get used to the idea that the world was going along. Then he realized that was what mortality meant. It meant that the world would move along quite well without him, just as he went on when his parents died and as his parents continued their lives when their parents passed on.

That was the nature of life, that death played an essential part in it. It was so stupidly obvious that he wondered why he had such a wild sense of a newly discovered and precious philosophical gem. It was the oldest bit of philosophy in the world, yet it was ever new to each person facing it. Death was quite common, but it was going to play a big and unique part in his life.

He was going to die. And the world was going to move along and forget him. What to do? Should he tell his wife? His children? Knowing himself, he knew he would have great difficulty burying this deep within his breast. He had no real friends in whom he could confide in such a situation. As an easy-going man, he had many acquaintances and he could hold his own in an animated, happy conversation. He could be, and was, a very entertaining personality. Yet he had no real and close friends because he had never felt the need to seek out binding relationships, except for the one with his wife. He never felt the need to need people. He never sought out people with whom to share his deepest thoughts, greatest fears and most piercing envies. So in a situation like this he found himself friendless in the true sense of the word.

Oh, there were many people who thought of him as a friend. Friends who would be shocked, who would be able to sympathize and even empathize with him in this awful situation, but there were none, except for his wife, to whom he felt he could turn for meaningful solace.

He went into a slough of despondency, full of self-pity and anger about his condition. "Why me?" was his constant thought. He had not been such a bad person. He did not deserve this fate. He would walk past the tennis courts and look with hot-eyed envy and anger at people bouncing happily around the courts, as he had done only the previous year, and his heart was filled with evil thoughts. By what right did they enjoy the health denied him? Why me? Well, why not me? And there was no response.

He considered suicide. In that way he could end the fear and cut off any possibility of the pain and distress that would accompany the inevitable illness. He would relieve his family of the burden of caring for a cripple, and he would not have to hear the half-felt good wishes of his friends and relatives. After all, suicide under such circumstances was a rational approach to the problem.

He thought of never seeing his children and grandchildren again and he was shattered. Stupid! Just because your life is being cut short, do you have to cut it off even shorter? How would his family handle the guilt, fear and shame of having a suicide in the family? Especially the suicide of the pater familias, the rock upon which his family had rested. Suicide stopped being a viable option. He was grateful, because he wasn't sure he could carry it off effectively. Poison, pistol and noose each had its drawbacks and he was revolted at the idea of a failure that could leave him crippled but aware.

Mixed with this regret, fear and anger was guilt. Was God punishing him? Perhaps his own lusts, his own life style had brought on this deserved fate. After all he had consumed mountains of beef, an expanse of eggs, and oceans of sweet ice cream and he had given himself up to rages of frustration over matters of very little real consequence. So he had the answer to his query, "Why not me?" He always had known that life had no intention of being fair and that on the whole he had taken more out of the pot of life's good things than he had put in. He smiled at the thought that there were so many things out there ready to kill him: polluted water, polluted air, cholesterol, and unknown chemicals and carcinogens. Now they had to stand in line to get at him.

While the thought that everyone was really dying came to him, he got little comfort from that bit of philosophy. He was still despondent. So like every prudent middle class man, he prepared for death by getting all of his financial and personal records in order. He took his will out of the vault and reread it. While the provisions held up pretty well, he could see that a few changes in bequests were in order. He would leave the temple a bit more and eliminate the amount to the American Civil Liberties Union. They had become a bit of a pain in the butt recently and this was a good time to punish them. His arrangements for his wife and children were in accordance with the latest tax law provisions, so no major revisions were required there.

He assembled all of the records dealing with his worldly goods. He sorted out all of his life insurance policies and made detailed lists of all of his assets, including the gold watch his father had given him when he reached forty. He noted that he should designate who was to get what from his extensive, if somewhat inexpensive, art collection, his cameras, his coin and stamp collections. What a lot of material things he had let clutter up his life! That was something to remind his children.

He knew why he was doing this. He had worked hard all of his life and he wanted his possessions to go to people he loved. If he died and some of his assets went astray or were lost to the family, it would kill him.

He checked through his records to find the deed to the family plot. He wondered if he really wanted to permanently reside in the hinterlands of Brooklyn. Would anyone visit him there? His parents and uncles were all interred there, so his generation of siblings and his children and his cousin's children might visit at times. As for the next generation, who cared? Besides, will I know whether they come or not, he thought. He recalled that when he visited his parents' graves, he always put a pebble on the headstone, following Jewish custom. I wonder why, he mused. If they could see the pebble, they could see me, so why bother with the reminder? Is it so the other visitors will spot your evidence of filial devotion? He made a mental note to check this out with his rabbi.

What would the learned rabbi think of him if he were to request that he be cremated, against Jewish law? Horror-stricken? Disgusted? Would he refuse to participate in his memorial service? Another mental note of something that needed further checking. Dying was not going to be such a simple matter; there were so many details to be taken care of.

But he did want to be remembered with affection and respect, if possible. So he decided to write an ethical will to leave as part of his *yerisha,* his legacy. Like a good academic he engaged in research and read about ethical wills from the Bible to the Talmud to Shakespeare's Polonius. Then he proceeded to write a long, somewhat lugubrious and redundant document admonishing his children to do a host of things they would have no intention of doing. But it was fun. He got a chance to emote unabashedly, engaging in high-flown King James language and stealing a lot of lines from medieval scholars.

With all of these tasks completed he rested and wondered what else could he do. He realized that there were many people who had been good to him, helpful and kind, and whom he had never really thanked. So he started to write a long series of missives to each of his friends, relatives and early mentors who were worthy of such expressions of gratitude, thanking them for their many kindnesses and indicating that he had decided to take care of this obligation while there was still time. That stopped him. Would they not all suspect that he was seriously ill and departing imminently? They were not so stupid and insensitive as to overlook this. So he wrote the letters, sealed and addressed each one, but put them all away with his ethical wills—the newest one and also the earlier drafts he hated to throw out. His son would be assigned the task of distributing these letters. At the funeral? So that they would remember, with a sob, what a fine fellow they had lost? Perhaps not. At the *shiva,* the wake, would be okay, too. Then they could read and compare his immortal prose. What a sobbing would arise! It would be a three-handkerchief night and certainly would add a unique flavor to the occasion. He thought of his wife's reaction to this maudlin proposal and decided that his daughter would mail them some time after the shiva.

The death notices in the papers had been fascinating him recently and he read them now with greater care, being particularly mindful of those who died of his ailment or close to his age bracket. He read the special announcements of praise and sorrow at the passing of some well-beloved or generous benefactor and he wondered how his would read. Why leave it to chance? With all that would be on the heads of his family making all of the arrangements, who could expect them to formulate a suitable announcement? Would they do him justice? Would they cite all of his achievements, his memberships, his many fine qualities and his modesty? So he drafted several notices to be dispatched to the main newspapers in the area. While he was at it, he prepared one for the professional journal and one for each of the alumni newspapers he received. As he reviewed his polished phrases and newly-coined clichés, he was pleased that he was so low key and so modestly sincere in his depictions of the dearly departed. Some parts of dying could be fun if properly attended to. He made another mental note to write a message to his son, permitting him to make some minor revisions in his deathless prose.

That brought him back to the funeral again. What would the rabbi say about him in his eulogy? He always admired the rabbi for the brilliant way he could weave a full tapestry describing the life and virtues of the dearly departed based on the few strands of information stammered out by the bereaved family. He could do this even without knowing anything about the deceased until that moment. But it wouldn't hurt to help, to jog his memory about this sterling supporter of the temple. So he drafted his own eulogy. After all, he had no need for research, just a humble retelling of the simple laudatory facts. He was careful to mention every service, some imaginary, some still just contemplated, that he had rendered for the temple in the last three decades. He mentioned, not too briefly, his illustrious career, his contributions and donations and his many awards and certificates.

His military career presented a problem that he solved by stating that through sheer military merit he had risen to the rank of private. He praised his wife and children and mentioned some of the *yichus,* the accomplishments, in his family several generations back. He looked it over. It was not bad, for a start. The rabbi could build on it in his own inimitable fashion. He typed it over and made a copy. Perhaps the local newspaper could use it as the basis of an interesting article.

He read an article on how to tape a "Living History" and decided to leave such a taped history for his grandchildren. He talked at great length into the tape recorder, telling how life was different when he was a boy. He spoke lovingly about the trolley cars, the horse-drawn delivery wagons, the burly iceman who delivered real ice and the drip pans under the icebox. He talked about how life had been so difficult without penicillin, dishwashers, TV and scotch tape. He described his checkered but successful career with pride and delight. He went on and on, enjoying every moment, as he thought of them listening wide-eyed as this ancient mariner told of olden times.

He tried to develop, orally, the complex family tree, but this confused even him. So he created a massive chart to go along with and illustrate the tape. Then he thought that if either of his children took the time to painstakingly follow his complex descriptions of the relationships of relatives, it would be a compliment to his or her filial devotion, if not to his good sense. Who cared that Tante Sura had married twice, first to one-eyed Lazar and then to Velvel the Horp? Would anyone even know that *horp* meant hump in Yiddish? The fact that Sura and Velvel's grandchildren, whom no one had ever seen or written to, may now live in Vancouver was of slight interest. When this project was finished (although he fully intended to go back and clarify some of the lines on the chart), he decided to leave tapes for special occasions. So he taped messages, clearly labeled, to be played in public for the family at events in the future, such as his son's wedding, the bar and bat mitzvah receptions of his grandchildren and the fifth and tenth anniversary of his death. Since these dates were now getting close to the date of the start of the 21st century, he taped a message of greeting to be played on the Chanukah just before that event. In passing, he added a few tapes to be played at Passover seders during intervening years. He fondly gazed on the rather bulky collection. He could not think of any other suitable occasions for which to make a tape. He made a mental note to consider converting all of these to videotape, though that would require assistance of another person and his secret would be out.

He was almost finished, but he still didn't feel ready for his fate. Would God renegotiate? He thought he had made a deal with God several years ago. "Don't give me anything, God, but don't take anything away." Now it appears that God was reneging on that deal.

He thought back to the days when being 70 was so unbelievably far off that one would be foolish to concern oneself with it. Now that it was upon him, it seemed that all of the prior years had flown by. Where had all the years gone? Why was he so trite? Life is trite.

As he finished the organization of his records and his letters of gratitude, he thought about the people who had hurt him, ignored him and irritated him, the fools, the clods, the *nudnicks* or idiots whom he had put up with for so many years. He owed them something. So he began to draft a series of zingers in which he cited one for lack of intelligence, another for lack of generosity of spirit and purse. He laughed happily as he sharpened each phrase and looked for the most devastating way to use his considerable vocabulary to hurt and deflate the acquaintances who didn't live up to his standards. He began to train his weapons on closer targets: a partner, a cousin or a brother-in-law who all deserved a bit of a reminder of how they had failed him. All of the incidents when he swallowed his anger or resentments in order to maintain the façade of family peace or avoid a career disaster rose up in living color. And he paid them all off, with witty, trenchant phrases and words designed to reach their weak spots. He was amazed how long-forgotten petty grievances rose up and poured out—thick, hot and sulfurous. He had a grand time constructing and re-constructing these missiles. That is what they were—missiles to be hurled to hurt.

But how could he have them delivered? He could not send them now because he was not willing to take the expected flak, especially in his weakened condition. Well, he could address and stamp them and request that his executor mail them out as one of the first orders of business. He laughed aloud he thought of these paper bombs reaching and going off in the face of his victims. That would serve them right! But suppose they hid their chagrin and said nothing to anyone? The public as well as the private humiliation he intended would not be possible. So he decided to photocopy each one of the letters. He would place them with someone who would make them all public, at a strategic time, so that all of the world, his world anyway, would know of his true feelings about these miscreants. In passing he wondered why he had withheld such feelings. Was he just angrily leaving the world with a parting and Parthian shot?

Now that he had gotten this off his chest, he felt much relieved. He looked at the carefully typed letters in their neatly addressed envelopes and considered. There was enough pain in the world. Did he have the right to add to it? Would it do any good? They wouldn't believe that his opinion was valid. They would only think that the fear of his impending death had unhinged him and his memory would be besmirched. He quietly placed all of the zingers into his fireplace and lit a match. As they burned, he smiled. It would have been worth it just to see their faces! Well, they will tell happy lies about me at the funeral, so I owe them the same hypocrisy.

He felt much better after this cathartic release and venting of some of the fierce rage he felt over the bad deal he thought he was getting.

He gathered all of his papers and placed them in a large labeled red envelope. He went to the bank and reexamined his vault papers. He checked off all of his lists. There was a niggling feeling that there must be something else he should be doing, but it didn't come to him. He had done all he could to prepare for the inevitable. Many of his relatives who had gone to the camps and the chimneys were not given such a grace period. So perhaps he was lucky to have a warning and to learn to use his time to the utmost.

Suddenly he realized how calm he felt. Death was not so fearful after one had time to adjust to the idea of total separation from the world as he knew it. Perhaps death was just another interesting adventure that would make grist for his mill of story telling. He wasn't resigned, just accepting of his fate. Thrashing with terror and useless recriminations did nothing to assuage his feelings and simply threw a fearful burden on his loved ones.

All done! For the first time in months he felt at peace. Now it was just a matter of taking one day at a time; that is the only way God allocates our days to us anyway. He would spend each of these last few golden coins in the most fruitful and enjoyable way he could.

Was he really ready? When is a person really ready? He was still alive and as long as he was, he would quietly wait for the *Malach ha-Mavet,* the angel of death, and hope for the best. Perhaps the angel will be late. Perhaps he will even overlook him.

He'd wait for the answers to his questions.

Old Buddy

For such a crowded place it was singularly lonely. The sun shone down with a watery gray light on the endless rows. Silence, deep velvety silence, was the first overpowering impression. Nothing moved, nothing made any noise. Even the trees stood quietly and refused to sigh with the wind.

He wondered why he had come, but he really knew. He owed them something. He had never visited them in all these long years, even though he had planned to so many times. Now that age was catching up on him, he was afraid to delay any longer. Besides he might be facing them sooner than he would like.

The rows of crosses and Stars of David stretched into the distance. In mathematically correct and proper military order they stood smartly to attention as he passed. How precisely they lay! He smiled as he recalled their ragged formations when they were alive and tired. The army finally got them to line up and stay lined-up properly. The green lawns and the graves themselves were meticulously trimmed, a sea of green carpeting the landscape. The nation honored its dead better than its living. How pleasant are your valleys, my old buddies.

He coughed into his cigarette butt and looked for someplace to throw it. He couldn't bring himself to desecrate the cool green ground, so he crumpled and field-stripped the butt, scattered the tobacco and put the bit of paper into his pocket. How many years since he had policed a butt that way?

Consulting the map they had given him at the office, he walked down the stone paths to the proper section. He then began to carefully read the markers. How young they all were! This one was 18, the other 19, then two 20's and another 19, none in this row was older than 25.

How long had it been? More than 45 years ago. A lifetime, he thought. But on second thought, not a lifetime to them. It was ancient history to him. He adjusted his paunch, lit another cigarette and wheezed along to the next row.

There it was, the section devoted to his battalion. The names came back as he read them aloud: Whittier, Porter, Wilmot, Panzer, Licari, Newman, Papenfuss and on and on. It was peculiar that he always thought of them by their last names. But that was the way that the army referred to them and so that was how they referred to themselves. So many markers, so many names, so many gone. Almost half of the battalion lay there.

He really couldn't recall their faces. Just their laughter, their jokes and the way they all loved each other. He had loved all of them, yet they were only anecdotes in his mind, tales and pictures without faces. The markers carefully noted rank—Sergeant, Corporal., Technician 5th class, Lt. One and Loo-ie Two—as though it really mattered to the dead what bits of brass had hung from their uniforms.

In most cases he remembered where they died, and how they died. But he wasn't sure he knew why they died.

Did so many die in that one six-month period? What a blood-bath! And then we gave the land back to them so they could out produce us in cars, cameras and chemicals. He wondered aloud what his old buddies would think of the situation today.

Suddenly he was aware of them. He saw Wilmot first. The sight of his lanky frame and lopsided grin caught him like a hammer blow under his ribs. How young, how lithe and healthy he looked! It was natural that Wilmot would be first. He had been his best friend and had gone from basic training through all of combat with him. Well, not all of combat. Wilmot had fallen about three months before the end of the bitter campaign.

Wilmot laughed, "What do you mean 'fell'? I was pushed. In fact, I was hammered down by an enemy artillery shell. Who the hell are you?"

"Ross, I'm Ross, Wilmot".

"Oh, Mr. Ross," said Wilmot, "I knew your son, or was he your grandson?"

"What are you yakking about?" asked the visitor. "I'm Ross, your buddy, Ross. We were in the battalion together till we went through that terrible firefight.

Licari, plump, roly-poly and disheveled as usual, appeared next to Wilmot and both stared at the visitor. Licari said to Wilmot, "The voice is familiar. It may be him."

"Ross," said Licari, his doe eyes glistening moistly. "What the hell happened to you? You're gray. You're fat. You're an old man!"

"The years happened to me," said Ross. "I've had a whole lifetime of work, sorrows and illness, while you guys remained young and unchanged."

Now it was finally out, his real reason for coming here. He wanted to berate them for his bad fortune and his poor aging and denounce them for their good fortune of being untouched by the passage of the cruel years.

"You stayed here unchanging while I went through tragedy and disappointments and illnesses. I've changed, on the inside even more than on the outside. I don't laugh the way we used to. I'm old and I'm sad."

"Oh, we were really the lucky ones," said Wilmot, sarcastically. "I never went back to my young wife, but you went back to yours."

Then Papenfuss, large, slow moving and as gentle as the cows his father raised, popped up to cry out, "I never even got married. In fact, I never really had a real date in my young life. I was really gypped by the war."

Ross defended himself. "You were really lucky. You died as heroes, young and brave and smiling. I always remember you all as smiling, while I'll die as a failure."

Licari turned his dark quiet eyes on him and said, "You had the pleasure of holding a child of your own against your chest. I didn't. You watched them grow, and even if they turned out differently than you hoped, you had the years to dream and the years to caress them. We didn't. You may even have grandchildren. Our lines ended with us."

Then Newman appeared. Tall, grave as always, mature beyond his years, he asked, "What did you do for a career?"

Ross mumbled about being an executive until mandatory retirement had cut him off from that life. Newman said, "I wanted to be lawyer and a judge, like my father. Until he died, he still kept a place for me in his office. But we were never able to be real partners."

Then Whittier and Porter appeared, paired buddies as they had always been. They had even died the same instant when their tank had been pierced by Tiger tank shell. "I wonder how we would have turned out?" asked Whittier. "I know I wanted to write, especially stories. I wonder what great novels or movie scripts were lost that day?"

Porter, in his quiet laconic Connecticut tone said, "I was always interested in research. Do you think I had a chance to find the fabled cure for cancer or polio?"

Ross was not about to tell Porter that someone had found, not a cure, but better, a preventative for the dreaded polio many years ago.

Wilmot, an honest friend as always, was the first to ask "What do you want with us? Why did you need to call us up? Why did you wait so many years?"

Ross stood silent for a few moments, then said, "I really don't know. I just needed to see you all again. I needed to be reminded, to believe, that I once was young, vigorous and as optimistic as you seem. Were we all so strong, so bursting with life's juices?"

Newman said gravely, without anger or animosity, "Bull! We spilled our life's juices on a strange land and here we lie, mostly forgotten and rarely visited. As for our optimism, it was a snare and a delusion. We had no futures, only we didn't know it. We gave away all of our days for a vague promise and even vaguer national interest. Weren't you better off?"

Ross flushed, sucked deeply on his cigarette, and cried out, "No, my life in the last years has been a hell. I am estranged from my family, my body has betrayed me and I live on the charity and sufferance of impersonal institutions. I miss you guys so much. Give me back my youth!"

"You're crying again," said Panzer. "You always were a crybaby. Remember how our family and friends cried over us when we didn't return. My mother cried her heart out over the years and I know it shortened her life. Do you know that our parents never got over the loss of a son? No one had to cry over you!"

"Yes," defended Ross, "but at least you went quickly. One thing after another is going wrong with me. I am filled with fear and pain all of the time. We have machines now that keep you in the twilight of a living death, a limbo that never ceases. The families cry and cry and there is no end. I don't like the way things turned out and I want to have my youth back!"

"We can't do that," said Whittier. "The same unknowing stroke of fate, the meaningless random violence of the field, left us here and permitted you to go on with your life, your plans and your hopes. You, in your own way, were as much a victim of random fate as we were. Do you think you were doomed to live?"

"I thought I was the lucky one," said Ross, "and for years I felt so guilty about you guys. Almost as though I had left you, had abandoned you to your fates. I couldn't shake the feeling."

"But then as the years grew longer and more gray, I wasn't so sure. We found that we had poisoned the water and the air. The wonderful things, like butter and steak, which we loved and ate with such gusto, we learned were bad for us. Even the sun, the blessed sunshine, is a killer."

"I kept thinking of you as you were—strong, fit, ready for anything, almost noble, and always laughing. Then I wondered why I had been selected to survive. I finally figured it out. I was the loser in the lottery. You were really lucky. You died as heroes, young and brave and smiling, I always remember you all as smiling, while I'll die as a failure."

"Do you honestly believe that?" asked Wilmot.

"Yes," responded Ross. "You got the better of the deal."

"Then look at us now, as we really are."

And the many skulls and parts of skulls looked at him with eyeless sockets.

Licari asked, "Do you still want to join us now?"

Ross hesitated, then coughed out the word, "Yes."

Then the skulls became faces again and they joked about how they would be able to make room for him. In such a neat environment, it would be impossible to create another place without disturbing the immaculate serenity and precise alignments of the rows. Some referred to incidents that did little credit to Ross' delight in their comradeship. There was even some resistance to accepting him. Ross waited anxiously. But eventually the group decided.

"O.K. Bring him along. We'll work out something as we always did. Share and share alike, old buddy."

Ross tossed his butt aside.

"Police that butt, soldier!" shouted Wilmot.

Ross bent down without thinking, responding to training decades old, and hastily grasped the cigarette butt. The group laughed with the unrestrained hilarity of youth. Ross flushed as he tried to rise.

The world disappeared into a black cloud rimmed with red. And he saw all of the battalion, lined up for the evening retreat. "Glad to see you again, Ross," said so many smiling faces.

Ross looked down and was amazed to see that his paunch was gone, his shoulders were straight and his arms were strong. Nothing ached or sagged. He walked with his body like a man astride a fine spirited horse. He now knew why he had come.

The caretakers came by and saw the figure slumped before the headstones. One commented, "Another one, overcome by emotions and regretful prayers. Why do they persist in coming even though it kills them?"

The Trip and the Traveler

How would you like to be able to live your life over again?

This "what if" occurs to most of us and has been the topic of many interesting, if inconclusive, conversations. Most people would relish a second chance. But I'm not sure I would. Now that my life is in its waning years, I'm not convinced that I would make better choices. I'm not sure I would reach a better destination in my life's journey. Being 21 today is far, far more dangerous than it was in my day.

When I was young, there was a sense of direction, an inevitability about choices, which seems totally lacking today. Change and chance were abhorred then. One selected a career line and hewed to it. One selected a mate and cleaved to her. Making a good living was more important than the concept of living fully.

One started one's life in school, then work, marriage and children followed. We were expected to stick with the choices we made. The trip was sovereign, not the traveler. One had a destination, not a destiny. There were few changes of career or mate. It was a rare person who struck off in a totally new direction in his career. Only a sharp discontinuity, like a depression or a family tragedy, was considered a sufficient reason for such actions. Those who did it often were considered shiftless and unreliable.

Happiness and self-fulfillment were not priorities. Self-reliance, responsibility and duty were the guiding tenets in one's search for security and comfort. Choices were limited, but clearly defined. We were no more high-minded or noble than the present generation. Not only did we not know better, we did not know any other way. That was the way things were. We expected less out of life and didn't demand greater freedom of choice.

The present generation is faced with a multitude of choices and options. If they don't like where the trip is taking them, they feel free to alter the direction. They can follow any whim, desire or principle. They feel that they are entitled to expect more out of life: more possessions, more satisfactions, and more high points. They feel bound by none of the conventions we accepted like docile horses. Just as they feel free to fly off to faraway Nepal or Cozumel, they feel free to fly away from mates, from careers, from family and religious obligations.

Once tightly held beliefs about love, sex, marriage, risk-taking, and how and where to live are all now transitory and ephemeral. Divorce and disillusion take center stage among the myriad of "meaningful relationships" that have no real meaning.

They feel that they have the right to change the trip and still arrive at a safe destination. I am not certain I could handle that freedom and the vast new expectations and still succeed in life. Nor can many I observe. They seem bogged down in a sterile desert of self-centered choices, haunted by the terrors of sexual freedom and AIDS. They are engaging in sex more often, but perhaps enjoying it less. They are discovering that, despite the gurus, they can't have it all.

We looked to the journey, while they look mostly to the feelings of the journeyer. The traveler takes precedence over the trip. They live in a culture more concerned with personal health and social relationships than with new ideas or innovative mechanical marvels. They take college courses like Yoga and oral communication skills, rather than mathematics and foreign languages. While they seem, or sound, like a more sensitive and caring generation than mine was, it is not surprising that we are losing our hegemony in the world market.

At my age it is easier to be calm about this. Life has lost a lot of its passion for issues. For those of my cohort who still can raise a strong passionate concern over events, I offer my great admiration. Life is simpler for me. Just to rise up in the morning and go to bed, without any new disaster to me or mine, is a victory for which I am grateful.

"A short life but a merry one" was one of the silly but romantic notions of my youth. But that choice is no longer mine. I've made the journey into a long life. Now I opt for a peaceful one.

So how long do I want to live? I recall a sergeant in Normandy screaming at our company, "Do you want to live forever?" I know he didn't. He is buried in Normandy. But how would I answer him today?

I don't think that whether I live or die can make much of a difference to the world now. But I am fascinated by life—by the ludicrous, intriguing, cruel, creative, noble and frightening aspects of man and nature.

I want to live, to keep on living, just because I want to see the next page in the news. Life is so full of new, awesome events, both frivolous and tragic, that I would hate to have my curtain rung down now. What will happen to my children? To my grandchildren? Who will be elected and who will be indicted? How will dances and skirts change? Will they finally make heart transplants routine and cure cancer? Will people actually live their lives and raise children in a space station? Is the earth truly warming up? I don't really care about most of these events, but I am curious about the cosmic and the comic.

Where the present generation looks within themselves for worth and justification, my generation found its worth within the journey. So give the youngsters their freedom. Choices are a heavy burden and freedom can be a curse. They will live in interesting and controversial times. May they, although I doubt they will, find the happy middle ground.

Give me peace to go on living, quietly and safely, now that my journey and destination are completed. I am affectionately but not passionately attached to the idea of living, at least until I become a burden to myself and to others.

A Happy Life

I have come to the conclusion that I have led a happy life. Despite my many tormenting illnesses and pains, which I won't catalogue, I sincerely think that in the face of my many hospitalizations, both as a child and as an adult, I have led a life filled mainly with contentment. Of course, no life of any interest is a steady diet of cheerful events. One needs the shadows in order to enjoy the light.

My work has provided a major source of my happiness. I have had a wonderfully checkered career, so that I never was bored by my job. What a dreadful fate it must be to go every day to a task that one hates. I would kill myself rather than do something like go down into the coal mines each morning. Some people might feel the same way about being a butcher, my first job. I never did. Every piece of meat was an artistic challenge and an opportunity to artfully carve the carcasses into useful portions of meat. No two pieces were ever the same.

When at the age of 17 I was in charge of my very own shop, I was filled with joy at my accomplishment. I was a boss! And I was earning much more than my friends, who had minor clerical or sales jobs. For the rest of my life I sought and usually found the routes to supervisory roles. Sometimes it took years, while at General Motors I moved up out of the assembly line ranks in months.

I had dreamed of being a teacher from my earliest days. Despite the burdensome years of night classes and the diversion of the war, as well as the forays into other business ventures, I persisted and eventually obtained the credentials to become a teacher.

As an aside, when Rose Shapiro, then President of the New York Board of Education, learned that I had rejected a supervisory job with General Motors at $23,000 per annum, a terrific salary in those days, in order to become a teacher at $2,400 a year, she asked to meet this *meshugenah,* this crazy man. I never regretted this decision, though, because I enjoyed teaching and I was good at it.

I never doubted that I would become a principal. In fact, while still a lowly per diem substitute teacher, I participated in a teachers' discussion about the fact that the principals were getting a large raise. I commented, "I think they deserve more." The other teachers were indignant. Why would I think that? "Well," I said, "I will be a principal some day and I want the wages to be worth the struggle to get the job."

My earliest principals looked at me askance. My classroom was always messy, colorful and full of laughter. Yet the children learned and were well behaved, even when I was assigned classes filled with so-called behavior problems. My first principal, Madeline McNulty McDonald, a disciplinarian of the old school, looked into my room regularly and always exited with a mournful look and a reminder to adjust the window shades so that all were even.

At the end of the semester she wrote in my evaluation report: "The man's room is too full of laughter. He will either be fired or he will become a superintendent." She also threw a party for me when I was promoted to serve in a Junior High

School (JHS). Years later I learned that she followed my career with interest because she wanted to see how I turned out. Regrettably, she died before I became a JHS principal.

Many of the secretaries I worked with also followed my career. I knew because they often wrote me as I was promoted, first to Assistant Principal, then Elementary Principal, JHS Principal and finally Superintendent. They usually both congratulated me and took some of the credit for my success. They were right in that. They were very helpful to me and often covered my ass when I made a mistake. I learned early on that the keystone in any good school is a good school secretary. The principal may be out for days with little effect, but if the secretary is out, chaos reigns. So even as a lowly teacher I would compliment them, flirt with them, bring flowers from our garden to leave on their desks before they arrived, and never forget one of their birthdays. In one large school where I had six secretaries, they would squabble over the flowers I left for them.

The secretarial staff could make or break a principal by the spin they put on his plans and the memos he sent to the staff. Mine, and I bless them all for this, were intensely loyal to me and would defensively support me when any teacher spoke unkindly about my programs or my supervisory techniques. I had to be careful not to let any secretary turn into an "office wife" with undue influence on my evaluations of teachers. I had been a boss for so many years, most of the time with workers many years my senior, so I had learned something about motivating and evaluating people.

I rose through the Board of Education examination system with great success and rapidity. I was restrained by regulations that forced one to stay a minimum of three years on any level before taking a promotional exam. I moved from sub to teacher in one year, from teacher, first on the Elementary School level and then Junior High School, to Assistant Principal in five years, from Assistant Principal to Principal in five years and then on to JHS Principal in two years. I never failed any of the exams I took, although many people failed three and four times. In fact, throughout my many examinations, 11 in all, I never scored lower than 10th on any list of many hundreds of candidates. Early in my supervisory career, I also came to the attention of the powers that be and was appointed to the prestigious Board of Examiners, where I tested many supervisory candidates.

All in all, my years in the New York City School System brought me great satisfaction. There were many days when I would silently say to myself, "Damn, I love this job!" I usually looked forward to going to work. Even as a child, unlike most children, I looked forward to the end of the summer vacation because I really liked school. So it is not surprising that I spent the major part of my working life within school walls. Even after I retired, I continued to teach adult classes.

While I had much professional success, there was also another hallmark of my life, albeit a sad one. I made friends easily, but I sloughed them off just as easily. This was in sharp contrast to my brother-in-law Jerry, who kept friendships for over half a century or more. My wife also has a similar, if smaller, number of loyal friends. Even though I often appeared to be arrogant, I liked people. So it was painful to lose friends, and that happened often as a child because we moved so frequently. I went to about 12 schools before I graduated high school. So to spare myself pain, I avoided deep friendships and rarely completely unburdened myself to a so-called close friend. (I noticed a similar sense of alienation in the army, when veterans treated the replacement newcomers with a standoffish indifference, so as to avoid the pain of losing another close buddy.)

I tended to be a loner as a youngster. I would walk all the way from the West Bronx to the East Bronx, including the length of the Botanical Gardens. The nickel I saved in carfare was applied to buying a used book. I never bought a new book until I went to college. Even then I bought as many of my texts as possible from the used book section of Barnes and Noble. (I was shocked as a child when my father invited me into a bookstore and paid the enormous price of 49 cents for a new book entitled *Bomba the Jungle Boy*, about a sort of teen-age Tarzan in the South American jungles.)

I was content with my own company. Though I usually was a good and facile speaker, I didn't feel the need to be constantly talking. And I didn't always feel that my friends would appreciate my innermost thoughts. I was the only one of my street-corner gang of 14 boys who graduated from college. I stubbornly continued going to night classes for 12 years because I had greater goals than most of my friends. They often mocked me and, I think, resented me because I seemed to look down on them. Perhaps I did. I know I never looked them up after the war.

I have no buddies from my school days, none from my meat cutting days, and none from the army or General Motors. Despite almost four decades in the school system, while I knew and was known by many, I have no friends from that period, except for a few rare professionals who needed my mentoring or training. They may have needed me, but I didn't seem to need them. I constantly sought what I thought of as "the real McCoy" among my acquaintances, but rarely found one. I have only been to two minor professional functions in the almost 25 years since I've retired. I have rarely joined organizations, and when I did, I was usually disappointed by the sterile activities and boring discussion. When I look at my pleasures outside of work, they were mostly done on my own. My work as a writer and editor for *The Light* tended to be a solitary activity. My one good sport was swimming, another solitary activity.

Yet I am content with this aspect of "loneliness." I do have a few close friends from my temple who give me emotional support and all the friendship I need. One of my fears, and I am given to many, is that many of these friends are now rapidly disappearing into their nursing home cocoons or their graves, and some day I will truly be alone.

For me, the most important source of emotional support and joy is my wonderful family. I think a large part of my happy life stems from my parents. I was fortunate to have parents who loved each other and who both loved me. I was a very sickly child and I must have been a terrible burden on two immigrants trying to make a life in a strange land while being forced to endlessly visit free clinics and hospitals to get the medical attention I needed so often. They never mentioned that I took away family wealth and attention needed by my siblings. They were wonderful role models and I grew up feeling that they showed me the way parents were supposed to behave. I think I behaved the same way in my relations with my own children. I also copied the longevity of their marriage, having been married now for over a half-century.

My father in particular showed me the way to live. I was fairly good as a meat cutter, but I was nowhere as good as he. He was good at everything he did, except accumulating wealth. He had such strength, honesty and dignity that he usually dominated any organization he joined. I felt proud when people would ask me if I was Joe Stier's son.

I remember in particular two pride-filled days with my father. One was the Sabbath after I came home from the army. I went to temple with my father and in front of the whole congregation delivered a talk about my days liberating Dachau. I was proud, but as I looked at my father, I realized that he was overwhelmed. The second occasion was when, as a Junior High School principal I invited my father to speak at the graduation ceremonies. He again was thrilled. I felt that I had partially paid him back for the disappointments he had in me in the past. He had always wanted me to be a lawyer who would run for public office. Looking back, though, he could have helped me achieve that goal by helping me to go to college during the day instead of letting me slave away for more than 12 years in night school. But I had persevered and I was able to show him that I had become a success in the school system.

It seems to me that I had a happy life because, although I had many awful days, they were swamped by many wonderful days with my family. Let me indulge myself by remembering some of those happiest days.

The day I came home from the Army was surely one. I will never forget the greeting I received from a treasured wife who now has cleaved to me for more than half a century. Since I had arrived in New York suddenly and unexpectedly and had outrun the mail, I decided I would surprise her. I raced to her parents' home on Schaefer Street. (Many war brides lived with their parents while their heroes fought overseas.) Without knocking, I adjusted my duffel bag on my shoulder and opened the apartment door into the small dining area of the apartment. Selma was eating and had a fork poised in front of her mouth when I appeared, filling the doorway. Startled by the apparition, she blurted out the immortal greeting of a wife: What are you doing here? Disappointed, I said, "Well, I'll go back and wait for a better greeting."

Then there was the wonderful and frightening day that we brought our infant daughter Emily home from the hospital. I must mention that the first time I saw her, newly born, she had matted black hair on top of a head that came to a point as well as a red face at which she clawed while shrieking like a banshee. No one had prepared us for what a newborn looked like, so I was horror stricken by this awful thing. I was afraid to tell Selma what our child looked like. But evidently she had already seen Emily. She said, "We aren't such bad looking people. How could this be our child? How can we take her home?" But by the next day her head had reshaped itself and her complexion was rosy pink. She was small, about five pounds, and her legs were scrawnier than a small chicken's. Selma was frightened to touch her for fear that she would break. So for the first week, it was my duty and pleasure to diaper her. We proudly displayed our child to the rest of the family. My father, a man with more dominance than empathy, wanted us to name her Esther or Molly, not very popular names at the time. Selma and I had already selected the name Emily, so I had the task of convincing my father that this name was actually a combination of Esther and Molly.

The day we brought our son Gordon home from the Guggenheim Pavilion's special clinic for premature infants brought us not only joy but tremendous relief. Gordon, born about two pounds, was already ten to twelve weeks old but still just five pounds, the minimum that they had set for the release of such small premature babies. We had lost one child and Selma had had several miscarriages, yet she was willing to risk another pregnancy. Despite our extreme care, she started to have labor pains at the end of the sixth month. We raced down to New York City from the summer camp in the Catskill's, but the regular hospital had no facilities in those days for such a small infant. My brother-in-law Ira, a *macher* [big shot] at Mt. Sinai, was able to get Gordon into the special experimental preemie clinic at the Guggenheim Pavilion. I still gratefully thank Ira for the wonderful gift he gave our family. Gordon has always been a sweet, obedient and beautiful child, and the many gifts we gave him were far less than the joy he gave me in just looking at and holding him as a baby.

My pleasure in Gordon did not supplant my deep love and affection for my first-born, Emily. It is true that I tended to ignore her while struggling with my career, spending untold hours studying for promotional exams and working on camp operations. But I was always secretly pleased by how many of my interests became hers: love of reading, gardening, photography and teaching. As she matured, I found conversing with her was a wonderful experience. She showed a depth of knowledge and empathy beyond her years.

Many of the happiest days of my life involve Emily's achievements. There was the day she graduated from Queens College and walked off with four major honors, including a teaching fellowship. I was joking when I said, "Why didn't you win the Woodrow Wilson Award?" and was sorry she was offended. I knew that she had accomplished a remarkable achievement, especially for a transfer student who had only been there for 18 months.

I remember watching Emily dress for her wedding, her eyes shining and filled with excitement and love. My heart almost burst with pride and love as I saw how regal she looked. When she smiled at me, I knew I was a truly fortunate father.

I felt even more fortunate when I dashed up to Boston to greet a new member of the family, my grandson Joshua. Emily was wonderfully excited and happy. I was stupid, though. Emily's mother-in-law Sally kept thrusting Joshua at me with cries of "Isn't he gorgeous!" I saw a nice looking child, but nothing remarkable. In the face of her torrent of joy, I said, "Well, he looks sturdy." She never forgave me for my cold response to her magnificent grandchild. She had a more valid evaluation of the child than I did. When Emily's second child, Rebecca, was born, I was more careful in my comments.

Emily's career also gave me great joy. There was the day she was honored by the Rhode Island State Legislature for her book, *The Elect*. I did not attend the ceremony because I was ill. But as I look back, I should have crawled up there no matter how ill I was. I have always felt guilty of depriving myself of a wonderful event and perhaps dimming Emily's pleasure as well. Perhaps it is just as well. My heart might have burst with pride as I saw my child so honored.

Since I first wrote this piece, there have been many other happy moments in my life. I felt great joy in seeing my son get married, and he and Beth have given me the wonderful pleasure of my third grandchild, Jessica. And my grandchildren Josh and Rebecca have both gotten married. It would take too long to list all the happiness that my family has given me, but they certainly are the main reason I look back on over 85 years and feel I have had a happy life.

At Point

I am "at point" in my personal life and I feel strangely exposed and vulnerable. I bring the term from my experience in World War II as the lead man in a platoon on armored reconnaissance patrol. In the lead tank of our tank destroyer battalion, it was our task to locate the enemy and draw fire so that the rest of the army could feel safe behind our defensive screen. While I may have seemed brave looking out of my tank turret, I was usually tense and terrified. For several months I was the most exposed person in the changing no man's land between two groups of well-armed men seeking to murder each other.

So now, as one of the elders of my family, I am in the front rank of our army of relatives. I once was the youngest and in front of me marched seemingly infinite numbers of grandparents, great uncles, aunts, parents, siblings, and cousins, while I brought up the rear. Time, the Holocaust and other tribulations have stripped and dissolved the vast rows of relatives that had marched before me. As the ranks in front grew thinner, the ranks behind me became fuller, as I was blessed to have children, nieces, nephews and grandchildren join the parade.

The complex skein that braids my family together is still forming behind me, while in front, it grows more frayed, threadbare and sparse. Whole battalions of cousins who should have marched at my flanks were shorn away by the Iron Guardists, those anti-Semitic fascists in Romania after World War I, by the chambers and chimneys of Treblinka, and by the Gulag. Only the sparse American branch and scattered splinters in Tel Aviv, Vancouver, Milan, Toronto, London and Santiago are still on parade.

Suddenly there is virtually no one in front of me. The vanguard of the whole older generation is gone and I am the older generation, shocked to find that at most family gatherings, I am the eldest. Now lightning is beginning to strike contemporaries; cousins, even younger than I, have fallen out of the ranks and my feeling of exposed vulnerability grows. It is like charging the enemy and becoming aware that a gap exists where there once was a vital comrade.

You look around and wonder where the army you followed is. Why is everyone behind you? It is curious and disorienting to meet mature people who were born after you graduated from college, to see a young nephew lead his child to bar mitzvah. While it is nice to be respected as the family patriarch, I keep thinking that it is not my role. That's my father's role.

My mother used to say, *"Der leben is a Cholim,"* life is a dream, and she could not understand where all the years went. I was impatient with her then. I felt it was nonsense. She should realize that she was old and that there really was no need for bathos. Now I am shocked to look down at my sleeve and see my father's hand and hear myself mouthing the same phrases that used to irritate me when my mother or father used them.

Now that I have changed from a thin irritable young soldier to a slow moving and portly grandfather, I find that I have the same irresistible desire to shout words of wisdom, warning and advice to those in the parade behind me; I find that I meet the same polite but unheeding response that I gave my elders.

336

I can't complain about being deprived. I have had my share of love and success, but I cannot accept the way the army before has vanished, and I look with amazement as well as love at the seried ranks forming behind me.

Do they feel safer, more protected, while I am still in front of them? Is that why we cherish the atypical nonagenarian, because he is still a buffer to blunt the aggressions of the *Malach ha-Mavet,* the Angel of Death? Does his survival make our survival more likely?

What I really miss from the vanished front ranks of my family is not just the assurance of their presence in case of an emergency, but also the unstinting, unquestioning acceptance and warmth they provided. They remembered me as a child and they still loved and forgave me. My children, like all children, have higher standards, and most of us are found wanting in their scales. At the same time, they have turned the tables and are full of advice I do not need and assurances I can't believe in.

I can recall my father introducing me to his friends. "This is my boy," he'd say, and his face would shine. My mother would brush a hair from my forehead and croon my name. I would brush them off because it made me feel small, but I was rejecting a kingdom of warmth and love. Freud says that one cannot be an adult until one's parents are dead. Perhaps this cruel dictum is correct, but it is a heavy price to pay for maturity.

At point, one should warily examine the terrain before you for traps and perils, but it is strange that one keeps looking back at the terrain that has been traversed. One cannot know what lays ahead in the unknowable terra incognita, so one looks back for comfort at the safe and the familiar, the closed chapter. And as one grows closer to the shade, the fires cool, but the timidity disappears also. The loss of the sense of outrage and desire is matched by the loss of anxiety.

As I look back, I find that I recall missed opportunities and bad decisions more than I remember triumphs and promotions. I recall the lost opportunity to show affection or understanding to a parent or friend; lost chances to spend time with the family under the seemingly relentless and important pressures to seek a livelihood. I trudge forward leading my parade, knowing that the next decade must be worse than the last. I am soothed by doctor's incantations that "we are all getting older," grateful for each sunrise that does not reveal a new physical disaster, another little death, another sign of the failure of a faculty or a death of friend.

It is like playing the film of childhood in reverse, as senses and memory decline. It is almost as though one were rehearsing the final cessation of all faculties. Since childhood prepared us for school and school prepared us for "real life," what is it that life and being at point, will prepare us for?